# The Beginner's Guide to
# CRYSTAL HEALING

# The Beginner's Guide to
# CRYSTAL HEALING

**Learn How to Energize, Heal, and Balance with Crystals**

## ASHLEY LEAVY

NEW SHOE PRESS

Inspiring | Educating | Creating | Entertaining

Brimming with creative inspiration, how-to projects, and useful information to enrich your everyday life, quarto.com is a favorite destination for those pursuing their interests and passions.

© 2022 Quarto Publishing Group USA Inc.
Text © Fair Winds Press 2017

First Published in 2022 by New Shoe Press, an imprint of The Quarto Group, 100 Cummings Center, Suite 265-D, Beverly, MA 01915, USA.
**T** (978) 282-9590 **F** (978) 283-2742 **www.quarto.com**

Copyright © Quid Publishing 2017

New Shoe Press titles are also available at discount for retail, wholesale, promotional, and bulk purchase. For details, contact the Special Sales Manager by email at specialsales@quarto.com or by mail at The Quarto Group, Attn: Special Sales Manager, 100 Cummings Center, Suite 265-D, Beverly, MA 01915, USA.

ISBN: 978-0-7603-8007-9
eISBN: 978-0-7603-8008-6

The content in this book was previously published in *The Beginner's Guide to Crystal Healing* (Fair Winds Press, 2017) by Ashley Leavy.

Library of Congress Cataloging-in-Publication Data available

Design and layout by Clare Barber
Photography by Alamy Stock Photo, Creative Commons, Getty Images, Ashley Leavy, and Shutterstock. Crystals property of Asley Levy, photographed by Sarah Maughan.

# Contents

# Introduction

*This is a book for lovers of crystals and students of the earth. It will help you take your crystal journey deeper than you ever could have imagined. You will discover how to truly connect with your stones in a personal way for deep healing, and for balancing the inner and outer parts of the self. It will also act as a guide for those of you who wish to use crystals to change the world through healing and service.*

When I was a young girl, I had the pleasure of spending many summer days with my grandparents. My grandma helped to instill in me a love of reading and writing while my grandpa nourished my fascination with the natural world—both of these passions have lasted with me to this day. During those special times I spent many hours with my grandpa in his study while he showed me his mineral collection and taught me about stones. I was fascinated by how such intricate beauty could be created by Mother Earth.

The desire to learn more about these earthly curiosities fueled me to pour over pages of rock and gem field guides, computerized encyclopedias, and books at my local library, but I always preferred learning from my grandpa. Although my grandpa approached minerals from a scientific point of view, this early introduction to crystals led to my own fascination and study of the mineral kingdom. I cherish those special days we shared together and am amazed, even now, at what a big impact they had on my life. It is in this adventurous, wide-eyed, crystal-loving spirit of my childhood days that I present you with the guidance in this book.

My own journey with crystals has taken me to places I never thought possible, and has been a truly important and transformational part of my life. Using crystals has helped me to develop my self-confidence, set healthy energetic boundaries with others, and heal past-life karma that was negatively affecting me. Because of these experiences I am now happier and more fulfilled than I was before I made working with crystals a part of my daily routine. I love myself and others more deeply than ever before, and I am grateful for every wonderful bit of this beautiful thing that is life.

It's time that I pay it forward and share with you, in the same spirit that my grandpa shared with me, a small glimpse into the world of crystals and their healing energy. It is my sincerest hope that the pages that follow will inspire and delight you, and that they will motivate you to create your own deeply meaningful and spiritually fulfilling relationship with the mineral kingdom. The following pages will show you exactly how to shift your energy and mindset using crystal energy, helping you to transform old habits and patterns, protect your energy body, and balance your emotions. I want to share with you the joy that I feel, and have felt since those summer days with my grandpa, and every time I hold a stone, pick up a rock, or sit quietly with a crystal.

Remember to be joyful in your journey, be playful, and listen to your inner guidance. It's your time to shine!

# How to Use this Book

*Crystals for Energy Healing is the ultimate guide to the healing properties of stones. It highlights the most important and useful attributes of these crystals, and shares simple yet effective techniques for utilizing the healing properties of crystals in your everyday life. This book is easy to use and has been divided into three sections that group the crystals into common categories of use, featuring the most common stones for each purpose, along with a few unusual or rare crystals that may be new to you.*

## Section One

In the first section of this book, you'll discover what crystals are, how they work, and some of the most common ways to use them. There are some great tips for those who are new to working with healing stones, including how to select, cleanse, and dedicate your crystals prior to working with them. You'll learn some simple ways to begin sensing crystal energy on your own so that you can tune in and "feel" what your stones can do for you. This section also covers the significance of different shapes and colors of crystals, and provides information on the corresponding zodiac signs.

 **Working with the zodiac is one way to harness the energy of your stones.**

## Section Two

This section is where you'll start to learn new ways to implement your crystal healing skills into your daily routine. You'll learn about using crystals in your sacred space and the power of using affirmations with your healing stones. This section also provides valuable information about using crystals for chakra balancing and other crystal layouts. You'll discover steps for creating crystal grids as well as instructions for simple but powerful crystal healing meditations and guided visualizations.

## Section Three

The final section is a sourcebook of stones and their properties. It is divided into three sections: Emotional Healing, Spiritual Healing and Guidance, and Shielding and Protection. These sections will help you easily find what you're looking for, but since crystals are dynamic and multifaceted, you will find that their properties often fit into more than one category. A great way to get to know the stones in this guide is to read about one or two of your favorite crystals, followed by one that may be new to you. In this way, you're not only deepening your connection to your old favorites, but you'll also create some exciting connections with new healing stones.

The crystals in the sourcebook each display a list of correspondences including the following:

- Appearance/color
- Current availability
- Physiological correspondences
- Psychological correspondences
- Associated crystals by color
- Keywords

The sourcebook descriptions also include a bit about the stone's geology and location, history and legend, and a detailed section on exactly how you can put the stone to good use right away.

When you're ready to take the next step on your journey, just turn the page, and start creating a deeper relationship with your healing stones.

# Crystal Basics

*Crystal healing has been used for thousands of years to shift the energy of mind, body, and spirit. Based on principles of both physics and metaphysics, crystal healing promotes positive change in the human energy field. In this section, you will learn something of the history of crystal healing, as well as how crystals can deepen and enhance your connection to your stones. You will also be given an overview of practical ways to select and use your crystals so that you can start to integrate them into your everyday life.*

# What are crystals?

A crystal is a mineral with a regularly repeating molecular structure. Most crystals form inside the earth during a process called nucleation, in which intense heat and pressure cause their molecules to form a three-dimensional lattice structure—like a blueprint. This geometric arrangement forces the crystal's molecules to take on the most stable form possible by repeating this pattern until the crystal is fully formed.

Having crystals in your energy field balances your body, mind, and spirit.

## Balance and Harmony

Crystals are more than just matter and molecules. The perfect, stable structure of a crystal represents the balance and harmony that most people seek in their own lives. As gifts from the earth, healing crystals are symbols of balance and perfection from which you can begin your own transformation into the whole, healthy, balanced being you're meant to be.

## Healing light

Because of their internal crystalline lattice, crystals are able to absorb and transmit light. This property, called refraction, allows crystals to draw in universal light energy, to reflect and refract it within their structure, and then transmit it back into the universe. The light energy is amplified and enhanced by the crystal's internal structure. All crystals are natural amplifiers of energy and assist personal healing by magnifying both the universal light energy that surrounds them as well as your intention for using them, and it is this that makes them such powerful healing tools.

## Good Vibrations

Each crystal has its own unique vibrational frequency, just as each person has their own energy vibration; the interaction you have with a specific crystal will be unique to you. You may find that you connect deeply with some crystals but not with others. Because of the subjective nature of crystal healing, it is best to use stones to facilitate energetic shifts, which can create an overall sense of wellness, rather than a symptom-based approach.

## The History of Crystal Healing

Crystals have been revered for thousands of years for their healing, divination, and other qualities by people from all over the globe including Chinese, Native American, Hebrew, Egyptian, Mayan, Greek, Tibetan, and Aztec societies. These sacred stones were first used as items of adornment, but the human relationship with the mineral kingdom soon evolved and ancient peoples began to recognize the energetic qualities of crystals. It is thought that as long ago as 25,000 bce, specific stones were used for health, love, luck, and spirituality. There is documented use of the healing properties of crystals dating from 1500 bce in the Egyptian medical text, the Ebers Papyrus.

## The Modern Crystal-Healing Movement

Although not yet fully accepted by modern Western medicine, the use of crystals as a healing tool has been growing in popularity for decades. There are now many people searching for modern holistic healing methods who feel drawn to using crystal energy to bring balance to body, mind, and spirit.

The modern crystal-healing movement first started with the readings of a famous psychic. Born in 1877 in Kentucky, Edgar Cayce channeled information about crystals, reincarnation, and other mystical topics, and was the first person to rekindle the human fascination with the healing energy of crystals. In the 1970s and 1980s, Marcel Vogel, an IBM scientist and the creator of the liquid crystal display (LCD), became one of the first to look at crystal healing through a scientific lens, drawing connections between the spiral structure of the quartz crystal lattice and human DNA, as well as recognizing the similarities between the silica composition of quartz crystals and that of the human body.

Healing crystals, including crystal skulls and spheres, were used by the ancient Mayans.

The liquid crystal display (LCD) screen was developed by crystal healing pioneer, Marcel Vogel.

## Crystal Healing in Recent Years

Crystal therapy has been become more popular in recent years due to the publication of books on the subject as well as the many classes and workshops now being held. With the Internet, people from around the globe have been able to connect and share their experiences with healing stones, further popularizing the crystal-healing approach.

# Ways to Use Healing Crystals

Maybe you read about the properties of a stone and felt called to have it in your life. You rushed out and purchased it only to have it sit around and collect dust because you're not sure how to use it. So what can you actually do with your healing crystal? Well, crystals and stones can be used for many different purposes—including healing, divination, meditation, energetic cleansing, intuitive development and astral travel, and personal growth.

## TRACK YOUR PROGRESS WITH A CRYSTAL JOURNAL

As you begin to dive in and use your crystals, it's highly recommended that you keep a journal of your experiences. For each new way that you use your stones, as well as for each new crystal, you should add an entry to your journal describing the stone you used, how you used it, and what your results were. This journal will help you to not only track your progress as you develop your healing skills, but it also acts as an excellent tool for discovering exactly how your crystals work best for you. Make time every few months to look back through the pages of your journal; you may begin to see patterns emerging in your entries. This journal is not only a tool for learning about your stones, but is also a powerful medium for self-discovery.

## Crystals for healing

Crystals are powerful healing tools. Healing stones balance and align the chakras and the aura. Crystal energy works on a subtle level, transforming the energetic roots of disease in the body. For this reason, crystals are a wonderful complement to traditional medicine. However, they should never be used to replace conventional treatments. While traditional medicine uses a symptom-based approach to healing, crystals are more integrative, creating energetic shifts that support physical and emotional healing.

## Crystals for divination

Crystal divination is the art of using crystals to help you tap into your innate psychic gifts in order to receive guidance on your life path. Crystal divination can take many forms including scrying, crystallomancy, and lithomancy. Crystal scrying utilizes slabs of stone like obsidian for gazing in order to view images and symbols that represent important concepts and themes in your life. Crystallomancy is the art of scrying with a crystal ball, typically made of clear quartz, which is used in a similar way to the obsidian mirror. Lithomancy, or stone casting, is an ancient practice of divining with stones. Stones are cast into a designated area, then read according to their properties, their relationship to one another within the casting area, and whether or not they fall within the casting area.

 Quartz crystal spheres have long been used for crystallomancy, a form of scrying divination.

## Crystals for meditation

Meditating with crystals is a powerful way to connect with their energy. They can be quick and easy or deeply intense sessions—create a meditation routine to suit your own needs. Hold your crystal while meditating to tune into its energy and create a personal connection.

 Crystal healers have used crystals for centuries to enhance intuition and facilitate mystical experiences.

## Crystals for cleansing

Crystals can also be used for energetic cleansing. They can be used to remove negativity energy, self-limiting beliefs, and worn-out belief patterns and thought forms. Your stones are highly protective when worn or carried with you.

## Crystals for intuition

Connecting with the energy of your stones during meditation or through divination is an easy way to develop your intuitive guidance. Some crystals can help you open up to universal source energy and connect with your spirit guides, angels, and animal spirits when placed in your sacred space. Stones can also be used for astral travel, dream healing, and more. Simply place the crystals in your pillowcase or on your bedside table.

# Sensing Crystal Energy

Learning to sense the subtle energy of crystals is an important part of working with your stones. Developing this energetic sensitivity helps you to connect with your intuition as well as enhancing your personal relationship with your crystals. The powerful energy of your stones can help you learn to tune into the universe around you. If you've struggled with sensing energy in the past, practicing the following techniques will help you to feel the energy of your crystals.

## Your Sending and Receiving Hands

The first step to learning to sense crystal energy is to discover which is your sending hand and which is your receiving. Although some ambidextrous people can sense energy equally in both hands, most people find they have one hand in which they feel energy more strongly. Typically, your receiving hand is your nondominant hand and it draws in universal energy. Your sending hand is your dominant hand (the hand with which you write) and moves energy out of the body and back out to the universe after the receiving hand has drawn it in. The process of sending and receiving energy is constant, but you can also consciously direct the energy flow, during healing and meditation, for example.

Learning to sense subtle energy, whether from a crystal or a person, is an important skill for all healers.

## Sensing Your Own Energy Field

A simple way to become familiar with energy is to learn to sense your own. Start by rubbing the palms of your hands together to activate the tiny energy centers located here. Then draw your hands apart and slowly move

them together, palms facing one another, until you feel the quality of the energy shift or change. Continue moving your hands together and apart to become familiar with the feeling of your energy.

## Sensing the Energy of Crystals

After becoming familiar with your own energy field, you can introduce a crystal. Hold a quartz crystal in one hand while performing the technique above. Notice any subtle differences in the way the energy feels—this is the energy of the crystal.

## Amping Things Up with Crystal Energy

If you find it difficult to feel the energy of the crystal in this way, hold a quartz crystal point in your dominant hand and point it toward the palm of your receiving hand. The energy in a quartz crystal moves from the base of the crystal toward the point. The termination, or point, should be about one to two inches from your palm. Begin drawing small clockwise circles with the crystal above your palm. Try to tune in and feel the energy where the circles are being drawn. You can also try moving the crystal point closer to your hand, then further away; note how this changes the sensation. Try making the circles larger or smaller, or even reversing the direction. How do the temperature, density, sensation change as you move the crystal in different ways? You may find it useful to make some notes about this in your crystal affirmation journal (see page 43).

 Crystals have the ability to amplify energy, so they are powerful when used to help you sense subtle energy.

## How Color Influences Crystal Energy

Another great way to start getting familiar with the subtle differences in crystal energy is to tune into the color vibration of your stones. Calcite crystals work well for this technique as they come in a wide variety of colors. Gather an assortment of at least three different-colored calcite stones and place them on the table in front of you. Pick up the first stone and hold it in your hands. Take a deep breath in, close your eyes, and tune into the stone's energy. After a few minutes, open your eyes, and set the stone down. Repeat the exercise with each stone, noticing the changes in energy caused by the different colors. Perhaps make some notes about this in your crystal affirmation journal.

The visible color of all minerals is created by the way that light reflects within the stone's internal surfaces.

# Selecting Your Healing Stones

Choosing crystals for yourself is an important part of developing a personal relationship with your stones. You may be drawn to purchase or work with a stone for yourself, for a friend or family member, or even for a client if you're offering sessions professionally. There are several methods to choose between: use your logic, your intuition, or a combination of both to assist you.

Once you've purchased your selected stones, you can also use these techniques for selecting the appropriate crystal for your purpose— whether that be healing, divination, meditation, intuitive development, or personal growth.

## Listening to your inner guidance

**Your intuition may lead you to work with a stone if you need its specific vibrational healing frequency.**

Occasionally, you may find you feel immensely attracted to a particular crystal. This can happen when choosing a stone from your collection or when shopping for crystals. When you feel called to work with a stone, it's usually because your intuition is guiding you to what you need most. It's important to listen to this inner guidance, as there is usually a good reason for this connection. This feeling can present itself in many ways—an inner knowing to use the stone or a strong visual connection.

**A common way to choose crystals is to select those that exhibit the properties you desire.**

## Choosing stones by their properties

There will be times in your life when you know you have something important and specific to work on—such as emotional healing, repairing friendships, or manifesting prosperity. Using the known properties of stones as recorded in books such as this is a useful way of narrowing down your choices. For example, if you're feeling energetically drained and lethargic, you may need a stone for setting energetic boundaries with those who are tapping into your energy field. The section of the Crystal Sourcebook on crystals for shielding and protection (see page 130) offers several options that will help set such boundaries, including spessartine garnet, heliodor, and pietersite. Once you have a shortlist of crystals to choose from, you can use a more intuitive method to select the right stone for your purpose. Use this method when purchasing new crystals or when selecting the appropriate stone from your collection.

## Trusting the Universe

There may be times when you don't have any pressing influence on your crystal choice. When this is the case, it can be fun to ask the universe for guidance on what you need most. One of the simplest ways to do this is to choose a crystal at random from your collection. Place a mixture of tumbled stones and crystals into a bowl or small pouch and place it in front of you. Take a deep breath in, close your eyes, and ask the universe to guide you in choosing the stone that's for your highest good. Select a crystal out of the bowl or bag at random while holding your intention to choose the stone that's most needed, and carry it with you throughout the day. At the end of the day, read about the known properties of your stone. Reflect on your day and think about how those properties may have supported you or influenced events that took place.

Learning to sense crystal energy helps you to choose the appropriate crystals from a group of stones.

## Tuning into Crystal Energy

Now that you know how to sense the energy of your crystals, you can use this skill to help you choose one to work with. Gather a collection of stones in front of you and place them in a row a few inches apart. Use your hand to scan the energy of the crystals, one at a time, and tune into the vibration of the crystal. While scanning the energy of each individual crystal, ask the universe, your guides, your angels, or your higher self if this stone is the best one for you to use at this time. For example, ask aloud, "Is this [name of your crystal] the best stone for me to work with at this time for [your intended purpose]?" There may be one or two that feel particularly strong or vibrant—these are the right crystals for you.

The Om symbol is a sacred mantra that represents the totality of consciousness and all that is.

A pendulum is an object suspended from a string that is used for reading energy and also in divination.

## Dreaming of crystals

On rare occasions, you may see a crystal within your dream state. This can be a powerful message from your subconscious mind that you need to work with the energy of this particular stone. When you wake up, reflect on the experience. Make some notes in your dream journal, if you have one, or on a piece of paper, and think about how you felt emotionally when you saw the crystal, what you were doing with the stone when you came across it, whether there were any symbols or archetypes present when the stone appeared, and so on. Dream symbols may include anything that seemed to stand out in your dream—an object like a rocking chair or a book, an animal such as a swan or an elephant, or any number of letters, numbers, or traditional symbols or signs (like a peace sign). Archetypes may also present themselves in your dream state. Archetypes may include deities, archangels, ascended masters, or representations of the zodiacal houses or tarot arcana. These symbols and archetypes typically have strong associations that can give you clues as to the potential uses or energetic qualities of your crystals and why the stones may be important for you to use right now. If you have the stone in your collection, this may be a sign to work with it; if not, consider purchasing it.

## Using a Pendulum to Select

You can use any type of pendulum for this technique, but a quartz crystal pendulum or a copper pendulum is recommended because of their ability to amplify and conduct energy. Hold the pendulum and ask it to show you a "yes" movement, taking note of how the pendulum moves—fast or slow, clockwise or counterclockwise, back and forth, or side to side.

Repeat this process, this time asking the pendulum to show you a "no" movement. Once you're familiar with your pendulum's "yes" and "no" movements, gather a collection of stones in front of you. Hold your pendulum over the first crystal in the group and ask aloud, "Is this the correct crystal for me to use for [your purpose] at this time?" If your pendulum answers, "yes," place the crystal aside. Repeat this process for all of the stones, setting aside any that your pendulum shows would be beneficial for you. You may choose to use this crystal selection technique when purchasing new crystals to determine if they are right for your collection, or you can use your pendulum to help you choose the best stone for your purpose from those you already own.

## Receiving Crystals as Gifts

One of the most beautiful ways you can be brought together with a special stone is if it is gifted to you. Receiving a crystal as a gift amplifies the energy of the stone because it is chosen and presented with love by someone else. When a crystal is given to you, pay special attention and reflect on why it may have been presented to you at this time in your life. It can also be useful to ask the person giving you the stone why they chose that specific crystal—their intuition may have played an important role in the selection and can give you valuable insight as to how to best utilize it.

 The energy of healing crystals is one of the most sacred and beautiful gifts that you can give or receive.

# Cleansing Your Crystals

Crystals have the ability to receive, store, and transmit energy, so they should be frequently cleansed of any negative energies. People often refer to energy as being "positive" or "negative," but really there is just energy that is either beneficial for you, or not. Cleansing your crystals removes energy that is not serving your highest good.

## When to Cleanse Your Crystals

If you work with a crystal regularly, it should be cleansed before and after use. Crystals that you wear in jewelry or carry with you but which you don't use for specific techniques should be cleansed about once a week. It's always best to use your inner guidance when determining how frequently to cleanse your stones. If you feel that the crystal is not working as well as it previously did, it likely needs to be cleansed. Similarly, if you have a particularly difficult day (physically, emotionally, or spiritually), you should cleanse this energy from your stone right away. The same guidelines apply if you encounter "negativity" from other people or your environment.

## Choosing a Cleansing Method

There are many techniques you can use to cleanse your crystals, but with so many options available, choosing one can feel overwhelming. Your intuition can play an important role in helping you select the cleansing method that's right for you and your particular crystal, so you should listen to your inner guidance. However, there are also some important tips to be aware of before diving in and performing some of the common cleansing techniques:

## Set an Intention for Clearing Energy

 When cleansing your crystals, hold the intention to remove energy that is not for your highest good.

No matter which cleansing method you choose, it's to hold the intention to cleanse the crystal and all energy from the stone that isn't for the highest your being. You should also intend to transmute any energy that's released from the crystal into positive the highest good of all.

When cleansing your crystals, visualize any energy that's released surrounded by white light to transmute it.

## Transmute Negative Energy

When cleansing your crystals, it is very important that you transmute the negative energy that is released from your stone into positive energy so that the negativity does not accumulate in your space. Visualization is the simplest and most effective method of transmuting negativity. As you perform any of the following cleansing techniques, visualize the energy being released from your stone and see it surrounded by bright white light. See this white light shine brighter, and watch it begin to break apart and dissolve the negativity released from your stone. See the negativity completely dissipate, leaving nothing in your space. Then visualize your crystal surrounded with the pink light of love and positivity. See this light expand and fill your space, pushing out any remaining negativity and transforming it into positive, loving energy.

## Crystal Cleansing Methods

**Water:** Water has been known as a cleansing agent for thousands of years. Clearing negative energy from stones with water is a common practice. There are several ways to do this. The most common method involves holding the crystals in your hands and placing them beneath a running faucet. You may also choose to fill a bowl with water and soak your stones overnight. Some people prefer to cleanse their stones in a pond or lake, river or stream, or even in the ocean, as they feel it is a more natural form of water cleansing. Using water can be a little messy and rather inconvenient if you need to cleanse a large quantity of crystals. Additionally, some crystals can actually be damaged by water. Soft or friable stones are most prone to water damage—including angelite, celestite, selenite, calcite, ulexite, turquoise, azurite, kyanite, and more. For this reason, water is not typically recommend as a frequent cleansing method. However, using water to physically clean dusty or grimy stones can be beneficial.

Water is the most common cleansing method, but it isn't safe for all crystals.

**Sound vibration:** Sound is an intensely purifying energy and its vibration has been used for driving away negative energy by cultures across the globe. From drums to gongs, to chimes, or even singing bowls, these instruments emit powerful, cleansing sound vibrations. Place your crystal or a group of stones on a tabletop or in your sacred space and sound the instrument several times. Continue sounding the instrument for at least thirty seconds, or until you intuitively feel a shift in the energy of your stones.

You can even try placing your crystals within a singing bowl—a metallic bowl, frequently of Tibetan origin, that is used for meditation and space clearing—to cleanse them. It can be gonged using a stick, or the rim of the bowl can be rubbed with the stick to produce an intense, cleansing sound vibration. However, if placing stones within the bowl, you should be careful with rough stones

**The strong vibration of a singing bowl is a safe and effective way to cleanse your stones.**

because the vibration of the bowl could chip them. Some singing bowls are even made from quartz crystal. These are much louder and more intense than the metal singing bowls and combine the energy of the sound vibration with the amplifying capability of quartz crystal.

**Cleansing visualization:** Your intention is one of the most powerful cleansing methods available, but only if you're confident in your ability to direct and focus energy. This is a simple and convenient cleansing technique because it doesn't require any supplies or materials. Simply hold your crystal, or a few crystals, in your hands. Close your eyes, take a deep breath, and slowly exhale. Visualize drawing universal healing light into the top of your head. See this light enter your body and move out of your hands and into the stone. Feel the energy surround the crystal and move into it, cleansing it of any low-frequency vibrations. In your mind's eye, see the crystal glow with divine light until you intuitively feel that the energy has shifted, dissolving any negativity or unwanted energy. When you intuitively feel that the stone has been cleared, stop the visualization. You can easily adapt this exercise for a large quantity of crystals by holding your hands above them and projecting the energy from your hands to all of the crystals in the group. This is one of the safest and most effective cleansing methods, one where you need not be concerned about breaking or ruining your stones.

# Dedicating Your Crystals

Dedicating your crystals is the act of setting an intention that they be used with love and light for the highest good of all beings. To do this, you need to state your intention aloud, say a prayer, or even perform a ritual or ceremony that communicates your positive intentions for the crystal. Many healers believe that the act of dedication helps to awaken the deva, or spirit, of the stone, and that it creates a sacred contract with this deva that you will use the crystal with integrity and positive purpose. By awakening the crystal deva, it will be easier for you to connect with the energy of the stone. This in turn will help you develop your personal relationship with your crystal and enhance the intuitive insight you receive.

## Crystalline Consciousness

Many healers think of crystal devas as living beings, but for others, it's difficult to think of crystals as having a consciousness of their own. When thinking about crystal consciousness in terms of the deva, most people visualize a small, fairylike spirit living within the stone. In a similar way, some people picture the consciousness of human beings as a tiny person controlling the mind and body from inside of the head.

Crystal devas were known as stone spirits to many ancient peoples. In many cultures, these spirits were considered to be guides that created connections between human consciousness and crystal energy, allowing the user to receive healing, wisdom, and protection from the stone. Some modern healers attribute the healing properties of specific stones to their associated crystal deva.

**Many healers think of crystals as living beings. You can connect with these stone spirits for healing and guidance.**

## A Ritual for Crystal Dedication

Begin by cleansing your crystal, your space, and yourself so that you begin the ritual in a place of purity. Hold your crystal in your hands and make yourself comfortable in a place where you won't be disturbed. Close your eyes and spend a moment tuning into the energy of your stone. When you intuitively feel that you have connected with its energy and are attuned to its vibration, speak your dedication aloud. You may write your own, or alternatively use one of the following dedications:

**Crystal Dedication 1:** "I dedicate this crystal to serving the universal purpose. I promise to utilize it for the benefit all living things, for I am a part of all that is."

**Crystal Dedication 2:** "I speak my gratitude for this crystal which has been placed in my care. I consciously intend to use this stone with love and light for the highest good of all."

As you speak your dedication, visualize the crystal filling up with universal healing light, glowing brighter and brighter with each word. When you have finished speaking, remain in meditation with your crystal for as long as you like. When you feel ready, slowly open your eyes and return to present-moment consciousness.

## Respecting and Honoring Your Crystals

After dedicating and blessing your stones, the next step is to show your gratitude to the crystal spirits by thanking the stones for working with you. The simplest way to do this is to speak your message aloud, thanking the stone for sharing its energy with you and for working with you for healing and balance. This message can be short and sweet or as elaborate as you like. The most important thing is to be sincere—send feelings of love and gratitude to the crystal and intent to strengthen your connection to the stone.

Regardless of whether or not you feel your crystal is a living being, has a consciousness, or is just an object possessing energy, treat this tool of light with respect. Crystals should be honored and thanked for their gifts and their amazing healing abilities.

 It is important to show your gratitude to your crystals when they provide you with healing energy.

# Crystal Shapes

There is a great deal of controversy in the crystal-healing community about which crystal shapes are best to use for healing. Some healers prefer natural rough stones because they feel the energy is stronger or more pure. These crystals—massive chunks of stone, geodes or clusters, or crystal points—have not been shaped or changed in any way. Other healers prefer to use shaped stones like tumbled or polished crystals or carved shapes. No matter which you prefer, it's helpful to have a variety of crystal shapes available in your collection so that you can gain experience in working with different types of energy.

Tumbled stones are smooth and rounded and have a very gentle energy.

Many healers prefer to work with stones that are just as they were when they were taken from the earth.

**Tumbled/polished:** These are rough crystals that have undergone a process where they are put into a rotating cylinder with a series of abrasives until the rough edges become smooth and rounded. Tumbled stones are typically inexpensive compared to mineral specimens like points and clusters. They are great for using in a medicine pouch, or to travel with, as they are sturdy and have no breakable points. The energy of tumbled stones is very gentle and is much less intense than that of crystal clusters or points. For this reason, these stones are great for people who are highly sensitive to crystal energy. Unlike a crystal point, which has a very direct and focused energy, the energy in a tumbled stone radiates evenly from the center of the stone outward. Water-worn crystals are a form of naturally tumbled stones, but they are dull instead of showing the glossy surface exhibited by tumbled crystals.

**Slabs/plates:** This shape is a thin slice of stone. They can be used for cleansing and charging other crystals by placing the stones on top of the slab.

**Rough:** These stones have rough, often jagged surfaces, and look just as they did when they were taken from the earth. Rough stones may be found as massive chunks, or they may have points or clusters of crystals. Most healers agree that the energy of these stones is very strong, so much so that it can feel too intense to people who are sensitive to energy. However, this intense energy can also be beneficial for diffusing energy and breaking up stagnant areas in the aura. This powerful vibration is very direct and works to create a rapid shift in the energy field of the user.

**Carved totems/fetishes:** Crystal carvings can be shaped into a wide variety of figures or symbols, which commonly include animals, deities, hearts, stars, and others. Crystals carved into the shape of a deity are especially sacred because they embody the spirit and energy of that deity. When a crystal is carved into these shapes they take on the properties and attributes of that figure in addition to the healing properties of the stone. For this reason, you can choose a stone that enhances the attributes of the figure or one that balances the qualities. For example, if you were choosing a carving of a heart, a stone like rose quartz would enhance the symbolism of love associated with the heart symbol. On the other hand, a stone like black tourmaline, which is more known for shielding and protection, would balance the attributes of compassion associated with the heart.

Heart-shaped stones symbolize love and relationships.

**Palm stones and cabochons:** Cabochons are commonly used in jewelry and have a flat back with a slightly domed surface. Palm stones are similar in shape, but both of the main surfaces are domed so that the overall shape looks similar to a bar of soap. Cabochons and palm stones are wonderful when used in crystal layouts because their wide flat shape helps them to easily stay in place when placed on and around the body. These shapes are associated with protection, as they look similar to a shield. These crystals are also connected to vitality and prosperity.

John Dee was an advisor to Queen Elizabeth I. He used his crystal ball to give her guidance.

**Crystal balls/spheres:** Crystal balls are perfect spheres carved from stone. This shape is known for enhancing intuition and psychic skills. The energy of a crystal ball is connected with wholeness and completion; it is a metaphor for the infinite. Spheres, like tumbled stones, emit gentle energy equally in all directions. They have been used for crystallomancy throughout history. One of the most famous crystallomancers was John Dee, adviser to Queen Elizabeth I. They are also a favorite of massage therapists, who occasionally use them as tools to massage the large muscles of the body.

Crystal eggs are highly collectable and make excellent acupressure tools.

Vogel wands are specialized energy healing tools that are best used where precision is required.

**Seer stones:** Also known as river-bed quartz, these are specially shaped stones, typically made from quartz-based minerals, that are used for scrying divination. To create the seer stone shape, rough crystals are lightly tumbled to give them a round shape and wear away any jagged edges. Then, the stones are sandblasted, which creates a cloudy appearance similar to etched glass. Finally, the stones are cut in half and the cut edge is highly polished, creating a window-like surface. This clear face can be gazed at and the viewer can look into the depths of the crystal. Unlike a crystal ball, which is often completely transparent and easy to see through, the sandblasted surface of the seer stones creates a backdrop for the inner landscape of the crystal. These stones are typically inexpensive and make excellent scrying tools for beginner diviners. In a similar way to crystal balls, seer stones can be useful for enhancing intuition and psychic skills.

**Eggs:** Egg-shaped crystals have a natural affinity to the concepts of fertility, creativity, and new beginnings. This shape is commonly used as a tool for assisting healers when scanning the aura in order to detect energy imbalances. Eggs can be used for acupressure by gently pressing the more slender end into trigger points on the body. They can also be used for crystal massage.

**Pyramids:** Pyramid-shaped crystals have a flat square base and four triangular sides that join at an apex. This shape has a history going back thousands of years that associated it with amplification of energy and intention as well as preservation. They are perfect for enhancing meditation and all spiritual growth work. Additionally, pyramids can be used to send distance healing to others and to project energy to other locations. They are also associated with prosperity and cleansing.

**Vogel-cut crystals:** These crystals are named after Dr. Marcel Vogel, a scientist and proponent of crystal energy healing. Dr. Vogel did lots of experimentation with crystal energy and determined that the energy of a crystal was strongest and most intensely focused when it was faceted into a wand with sides in multiples of twelve (12, 24, etc.). These wands are typically made of varieties of quartz crystal—clear quartz, amethyst, smoky quartz, rose quartz, citrine, etc.—and have terminations on either end.

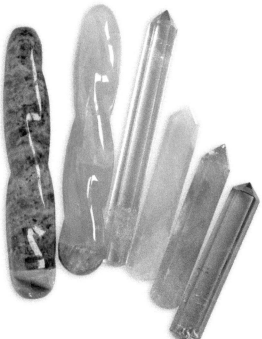

Vogel triangles are double-sided, with four smaller, faceted triangles on each side (pointing in opposite directions), which means that when looking through the triangle, you can see a Star of David shape. These are very powerful shapes and are typically reserved for very intense healing work such as psychic surgery.

**Massage and reflexology wands:** These stones have been cut and polished into a long, slender, wand-like shape. Massage wands are rounded on both ends, typically with one narrow end to be used for small areas like the face, and one larger end for use in larger areas like the back and legs, to help relieve muscle tension. Reflexology wands are quite thin and have one pointed end to be used for stimulating reflex points in the ears, and one small rounded end for stimulating reflex points in the face, hands, and feet. These wands can also be used on the energy body to open chakras and direct energy.

Carved crystal wands can be used in combination with traditional massage or reflexology techniques.

**Generators:** Crystal generators are used to draw in, direct, and amplify universal energy. They may occasionally form naturally, but are more commonly cut and polished into their characteristic shape—six equal sides and six equal faces that join to form a perfect point at the top of the crystal. Many healers use generators for sending distance healing energy, amplifying the power of crystal grids, and drawing energy into a healing room or sacred space. This shape is also excellent for promoting group cooperation and for helping people work together to achieve a common goal.

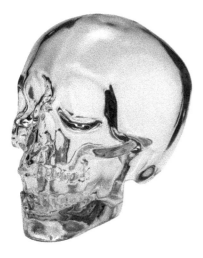

Crystal skulls have a mysterious history, but modern-day healers use them for wisdom and insight.

**Skulls:** Crystal skulls are becoming more popular each day and offer an interesting approach to working with crystal energy. Most proponents of crystal skulls believe that there are many ancient skulls. The origins and history of these objects is hotly debated, but if you can see beyond the mystery, there is much to be learned from working with them. Most commonly, they are used for channeling. Some believe that this information comes from the skull itself, while others believe the skull is simply a portal to connect with beings from other dimensions. Many people claim that the crystal skulls are here on earth at this time to assist with the evolution of human consciousness. They are powerful tools for enhancing meditation and healing work.

**Donuts:** These stones have been carved into a flat circular disc with a round hole cut out of the center. Donuts are frequently worn as necklaces by stringing them onto a cord. In Japan, they are used by therapists for a special antiaging facial massage. This shape is also known as a Pi stone.

**Merkaba:** Sometimes referred to as a double tetrahedron or as a star tetrahedron, the merkaba displays twenty-four faces and thirty-six edges. This shape represents balance between physical and spiritual growth.

Merkabas are the most powerful sacred geometry shapes and are used for spiritual transformation.

# PLATONIC SOLIDS/SACRED GEOMETRY SHAPES

These crystals have been cut into the five Platonic solids shapes. Plato theorized that all space in the universe, both positive and negative, followed the form of one of these five sacred shapes:

### TETRAHEDRON

Displays four triangular sides and six edges. Represents the fire element. Associated with confidence, motivation, and vitality.

### CUBE (HEXAHEDRON)

Displays six square sides and twelve edges. Represents the earth element. Associated with grounding, stability, and protection.

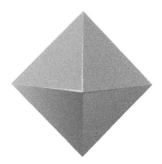

### OCTAHEDRON

Displays eight triangular sides and twelve edges. Represents the air element. Associated with mental clarity, problem solving, and intellect.

### DODECAHEDRON

Displays twelve pentagonal sides and thirty edges. Represents the spirit (or ether) element. Associated with spiritual growth.

### ICOSAHEDRON

Displays twenty triangular sides and thirty edges. Represents the water element. Associated with intuition, emotional balance, and psychic awareness.

# The Healing Properties of Color

Color has been scientifically proven to affect human moods and emotions. By understanding how color influences crystal energy, you will be better able to select stones for specific healing techniques, to balance the chakra centers, and to create positive emotional shifts.

You may use this information in several ways. For example, if you find yourself consistently being drawn to pink stones this may indicate that it is time for change and new beginnings, or it may indicate that you are naturally empathic and need support as you show your compassion to others. On the other hand, if you are offended or irritated by a particular color, it may indicate that you have something to work on in one of those associated areas. For example, if you really dislike the color orange, it may indicate that you need to find more emotional balance in your life or that you need to start expressing your creativity.

Alternatively, you may use these colors to help you select a crystal for yourself. If, for example, you'd like to get in touch with your spiritual aspect, then you may want to choose a violet-colored stone like amethyst or charoite to help you develop your spirituality.

The color of a stone has a great deal of influence on its associated properties.

# COLOR PROPERTIES

### RED
Passion, vitality, motivation, stability, protection, physical healing, instinct.

### WHITE
Purification, protection, sacredness, divine connection, meditation.

### ORANGE
Emotional balance, creativity, sexuality, transformation, inner-parts work.

### PINK
Compassion, friendship, new beginnings, empathy, inner-child work.

### YELLOW
Courage, inner strength, bravery, self-confidence, willpower, mental clarity.

### TEAL
Inner peace, harmony, tranquility, compassion, spirit guides and angels.

### GREEN
Love, compassion, emotional healing, growth, prosperity, abundance, physical health.

### BLACK
Protection, self-reflection, change, personal growth, shadow-side work.

### BLUE
Communication, truth, wisdom, self-expression, authenticity, integrity, justice.

### BROWN
Grounding, shielding, stability, inner peace, nature spirits.

### INDIGO
Intuition, psychic awareness, spiritual growth, mental expansion.

### GRAY
Balance, open-mindedness, dream work, dream recall, astral travel.

### VIOLET
Spirituality, personal growth, transformation, ascension, conscious awareness.

# Crystals and The Zodiac

People have been wearing and using zodiac stones for thousands of years, but in the modern day these traditional stones are often replaced with birthstones.

Birthstones are gemstones (both precious and semiprecious) that are assigned to a specific month. The modern list of birthstones was created in 1912 by the National Association of Jewelers in the USA. Many of the gemstones included in the list were loosely based on those traditionally assigned to signs of the zodiac. However, birthstones are not as energetically aligned with your unique astrological influences as those that follow the dates of the zodiac.

Since zodiac stones have a correspondence to the planet that rules over your zodiac sign, choosing a zodiac crystal rather than a birthstone is recommended, as it will work better in energetically supporting what you need. In some cases, these stones may be the same, but this isn't always the case. Wearing or using crystals for their zodiac correspondences will amplify the positive traits of your sign while working to balance its negative traits.

 **Zodiac stones are associated with the ruling planet of an astrological sun sign.**

# ZODIAC CRYSTALS

### CAPRICORN
Dec. 22nd to Jan. 20th
garnet, amber, onyx

### AQUARIUS
Jan. 21st to Feb. 19th
amethyst, bloodstone,
aquamarine

### PISCES
Feb. 20th to Mar. 20th
blue kyanite, blue
tourmaline, blue quartz

### ARIES
Mar. 21st to April 19th
diamond, smoky quartz,
clear quartz

### TAURUS
April 20th to May 20th
emerald, rose quartz,
pink opal

### GEMINI
May 21st to June 21st
citrine, tree agate,
rainforest jasper

### CANCER
June 22nd to July 23rd
ruby, fire agate,
sunstone

### LEO
July 24th to Aug. 23rd
heliodor, golden tiger's
eye, yellow jasper

### VIRGO
Aug. 24th to Sept. 22nd
sapphire, magnetite,
hematite

### LIBRA
Sept. 23rd to Oct. 22nd
boulder opal, obsidian,
fire opal

### SCORPIO
Oct. 23rd to Nov.
22nd yellow topaz,
labradorite,
black moonstone

### SAGITTARIUS
Nov. 23rd to Dec. 21st
turquoise, jet,
lapis lazuli

# Crystal Healing

*Healing stones can be used in many ways, such as in your sacred space, with affirmations, within a crystal medicine bag, for layouts, in crystal grids, and for crystal meditation. By testing different methods, you'll find some that suit your needs more than others. It's great to stick with these most of the time, but be sure to try something outside your comfort zone occasionally. Many of the following techniques can be combined to boost results. They can be used for self-care, or you can use them to provide crystal healing for your friends or family.*

# Starting Your Crystal Journey

It's time for you to start your exciting journey into the world of crystals and energy healing. Working with crystals is a subjective and deeply personal experience. Each person will use their stones in different ways. There are no right or wrong answers when it comes to crystal healing—there is only your experience. Work to stay present in the moment and be open to your experiences with your stones. Remember to stay focused and allow yourself to fully open up and connect with the many unique members of the mineral kingdom.

The best way to get the most out of working with your crystals is to use them each day.

## How To Use Crystals Every Day

There are many ways to use crystals in your day-to-day life. You can carry a selection of stones with you in your pocket or a small pouch, or you can wear your healing stones set in jewelry. Alternatively, place a small bag (or a dish or bowl) of stones in a prominent area of your home or workplace—or anywhere you spend a great deal of time. You may choose to create a small crystal grid or a geometric arrangement of stones, or add some special crystals to a sacred stone medicine pouch.

You can also carry out some basic energy healing by placing a stone on one of your chakra centers for 5–10 minutes. This will allow you to absorb the balanced, healing energy of the stone into the chakra. Perform this technique as often as you like. You may want to dive even deeper into your work with crystals by trying out a crystal layout, where crystals are placed on and around the physical body in order to shift the energy. Follow a layout or simply follow your inner guidance and intuition.

## Creating Focus and Clarity

Another way to dive deep with your healing stones is to tune into their energy during a meditation session. The following meditation can help you clear your mind and prepare for your new journey. This meditation works best when using clear quartz, rainbow fluorite, or golden tiger's eye stones because of their association with focus and mental clarity, but you can choose any crystal that you are intuitively drawn to.

Golden tiger's eye improves mental clarity and enhances focus.

# CRYSTAL MEDITATION

## What To Do:

1. Make yourself comfortable in a place where you will not be disturbed. Hold your crystal in cupped hands, close your eyes, and take a deep breath. Focus your attention on the stone in your hands; try to feel its energetic vibration.

2. Take a deep breath in, hold for a count of three, and slowly exhale. On your next breath, become aware of the crystal energy on a deeper level. Stay focused only on your crystal and your breathing. If you catch your mind starting to wander, return your attention to your breath. Take a deep breath in, hold for a count of three, and slowly exhale.

3. Continue in this way, allowing yourself to absorb the energy of the stone, feeling your mind focus on the present moment and releasing all other thoughts. Feel any distractions slipping away until you are only aware of yourself and your healing stone. Remain in silent meditation for as long as you like, then when you feel ready, take a deep breath in, exhale, open your eyes, and return to present-moment consciousness. Take a look around, allowing yourself to see what surrounds you but without allowing it to take your attention away from your connection to your crystal.

As you continue to practice, your goal should be to come out of the meditation and remain free from distraction for longer and longer periods of time. Eventually, you will be able to apply this disciplined approach to tuning into crystal energy under any circumstances.

# Crystals in Your Sacred Space

Your sacred space is your personal sanctuary and it provides a place where you can connect to the universal source energy so that you're able to recharge and rejuvenate yourself. It may include objects that are sacred to you and your connection to the spirit, such as statues, symbols, color energy, crystals, candles and incense, and uplifting artwork. Your sacred space is a place of personal power and strength for you, and your point of connection to universal energy, so whatever you choose, it is important the items are personal and meaningful to you. Think about the ways that you'll use this sacred space and what would best support you, and choose your items and crystals accordingly. Then, as your intention changes and grows, you can update the items.

Add items to your crystal altar that are meaningful to you—make it personal.

## Your Crystal Altar

The creation of a crystal altar is a simple way to pull all of these elements together in one small, convenient space. Choose an area within your sacred space where you will be able to stop and appreciate your altar regularly. It's wonderful if you can have a small desk or table to use for your altar, but a tiny shelf or even a windowsill is fine. Be sure to set an intention for your altar— what is your purpose for creating it? What would you like to use it for? Once you have a purpose in mind, choosing what to add to it becomes much easier.

You can bring some color energy (see page 33) into the space with the crystals you display, or incorporate colorful tablecloths and fabric to call in the properties associated with the colors you choose. Additionally, you can add things that are sacred to you—family heirlooms, statues, symbols, candles, incense, etc. You may also want to add something that is really sacred or beautiful to you like fresh flowers, feathers, or other objects you find in nature.

## Your Crystals

The most important part of your crystals altar is, of course, the crystals themselves, chosen according to the properties you'd like to call into your life. By referring to the Crystal Sourcebook (see pages 52–155) you can select those most relevant to you and your intentions. You can arrange the crystals in any way that you find pleasing, or you can further boost the energy of your stones by creating a crystal grid.

## Connecting with Your Inner Guidance

Some healers also choose to use crystal divination tools on their crystal altars. You may want to add a crystal ball, gemstone pendulum, or casting stones. When you're at your altar in your sacred space, your energy is focused and centered and allows you to clearly receive any messages that come through during your divination session.

Use selenite to protect your space and keep the energy cleansed and purified.

## Keeping Your Sacred Space Cleansed

Finally, it's recommended that you keep a selenite crystal in your sacred space. Selenite is one of the best crystals for space clearing, and keeping one atop your altar or in your space will help keep the energy free from negativity as well as calling in your guides and angels to keep the space protected.

# The Power of Crystals and Affirmations

Crystals are powerful, natural amplifiers of energy. When you combine them with the transformative abilities of affirmations, you have a winning recipe for positive transformation. Affirmations are conscious statements of your intent that help to co-create your reality. They are like messages that you share with the universe in order to communicate your wants, needs, goals, dreams, vision, wishes, and desires. When you focus your full attention on manifesting your affirmation statements into being, and you support that energy with crystals, you can create major shifts in your life energy.

## Programming vs. Affirmations

Some people practice the technique of programming their stones for specific purposes. Although this would seem to make sense at first, you may find this method to be a little restrictive when compared to using affirmations.

Programming your crystals gives them a specific and direct objective. When you program a stone, you're directing it to focus on only that one specific thing and nothing else. This can really limit the healing potential of the crystal. With affirmations, however, you're making a request of the crystal about what feels most important to you, without restricting the stone's abilities in any way. The crystal will often know best how to help you, and by working with affirmations rather than programming, you allow the crystal the freedom to work for your highest good rather than imposing your will on the stone. This is important because you may not always be able to see what is best for you or be aware of everything that's going on within your body, mind, and spirit, and the stone will work objectively on all areas of your being.

## Creating a Crystal Affirmation Journal

Using an affirmation journal is a simple way to incorporate affirmations into your daily practice, a place where you can keep track of your affirmations and manifesting work. The journal can be used for keeping records of the transformation and change you've been able to create in your life with each affirmation.

You can create your own by choosing a blank journal, one that will keep you excited and motivated to use it. You may also want to decorate your journal to add some positive energy and personal touches to it.

## Writing Your First Affirmations

Once you have your affirmation journal ready, the next step is to craft your first affirmation. Writing this affirmation states your intention to the universe and is a catalyst for personal transformation. Be sure to write your affirmation as clearly and concisely as possible, phrasing it in the present tense, as if you have already manifested it, rather than using the future tense. Stating "I will" or "I am going to" in your affirmations continues to push your manifestation of these things into the future rather than calling them into the present moment. By using the present tense, you are telling the universe that you are holding space for these things in your life and that you are ready to accept them now.

It's also important that your affirmation is framed in the positive, focusing on what you want to draw into your life, rather than focused on the negative. For example, rather than stating, "I don't want to be sick anymore," which focuses on illness, you should say something like, "My body is healthy and balanced," which focuses on overall health and wellbeing. Instead of, "I am healing the emotional pain caused by my divorce," which is full of hurtful memories and emotions, you should phrase your affirmation to read something like, "I gratefully accept new, healthy, loving relationships into my life," which is specific about what you'd like to call into being.

Writing your affirmations in your journal helps you to remember your intention clearly and to track your progress.

If you've written your affirmation to read something like, "I am not poor and no longer struggle financially," then you're placing your energy and attention on financial troubles rather than on abundance. A better solution would be to affirm that "I manifest abundance in all areas of my life including financial abundance, an abundance of love, and an abundance of good health." In this way, you shift your mindset from one of scarcity and poverty consciousness to an abundance mindset that calls in positive energy in all aspects of your life and enhances your ability to magnify that which you need most.

In this way, you manifest positive things into your life, rather than focusing your energy and intention on things that are not for your highest good. It is also recommended that you add the words, "This, or something better," to the end of your affirmation so as not to limit your manifesting potential. If you need some inspiration, you may find it useful to hold your favorite crystal while writing your affirmation. Think about the way the crystal makes you feel and about all of the ways in which you could be more aligned with positivity in your life, then craft your intention statement.

## Using Your Affirmation Journal

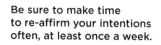 Be sure to make time to re-affirm your intentions often, at least once a week.

To begin using your affirmation journal, choose a crystal that's aligned with the purpose of your affirmation. Hold the crystal in your hands and speak your affirmation aloud. Feel the energy of the stone amplifying the power of your words, sending them out with focus and direction. This act creates a positive, energetic shift in your body, mind, and spirit. You can follow this process as often as you like, but making time at least once a week to stay active with your manifesting work shows the universe that you are holding space in your life for the change to take place.

Each week when you repeat the process, take some time to jot down a few notes about how you've moved closer to manifesting things relating to your affirmation. For example, if your affirmation is focused on manifesting good health, then write about any steps you've taken to improve this aspect of your life—perhaps include some notes about your sleep habits, your diet, any visits to your doctor, or general notes about how you've been feeling. Make an assessment about whether you feel you've improved, stayed the same, or if you've gotten a bit off track. If you haven't improved since your last entry, ponder on why this might be and what you can do during the next week that will help you.

You can also record any feelings or ideas relating to this area of your life. Hold your chosen crystal while reflecting on your week and allow the energy of the stone to help shine some light on how you're connecting to the transformative energy you're creating with your affirmation. As you go through this process each week, evaluate your affirmation to be sure it's still relevant to what you'd like to manifest into your life. If, over time, your manifesting goals change, be sure to write a new affirmation and choose a new stone to work with so that you are working toward things that are aligned with the transformation you'd like to create in your life.

Be sure to date each entry in your affirmation journal so that you keep track of your growth and progress toward manifesting your affirmation. The other benefit of dating these entries is that it shows you how frequently you're actually using your journal. It can also be easy to put off the things that you likely need to do the most, so check over your entries frequently to be sure you're staying on track with a regular routine.

## More Ways to Use Your Affirmations

Because combining crystals and affirmations is such a powerful practice, it's strongly suggested that you find additional ways to incorporate this technique into your life. You may try posting your affirmations on your vision board (a visual reminder of things you'd like to manifest in your life) or even chanting your affirmation during a crystal meditation (see page 48). You can create a crystal grid, a geometric formation of crystals used for manifesting, and place your affirmation at its center to add some extra energy to your manifesting practice. Or try writing your affirmation on a piece of paper and wrapping it around your crystal to charge it with the vibration of your intention. Carry this stone with you wherever you go to work on your manifesting.

**When you say your affirmations, hold a crystal that's aligned with your purpose.**

# Crystals and the Chakra Centers

The chakras are energy centers found in the body. The word chakra is Sanskrit for "wheel," as these centers are thought of as swirling discs of light energy. The chakras send and receive universal energy—they are a connection point to the world around us. There are seven major chakras, found along the spine, and countless minor chakras that rule different areas of the body, mind, and spirit. Numerous minor chakras also influence the body's energy.

The chakra centers create balance in all aspects of your being. When they are healthy and open, energy moves between them, keeping your body, mind, and spirit in a place of wellness, but because the chakra centers are in constant contact with the influences of external energy, they are in a constant state of flux and can easily become unbalanced. Unbalanced chakras can result in physical, mental, emotional, and spiritual problems.

The seven major chakras are vortices of energy that each govern certain aspects of the body, mind, and spirit.

## Aligning the Chakras

Healing crystals can be used to bring the chakra centers back into alignment. Typically, stones are chosen for each chakra center based on their associated color. By bringing the color frequency of the stone into its corresponding chakra, the energy center is strengthened and balanced. The healing energy emitted by the crystal helps to realign the energy of the chakra, creating harmony in the energy field.

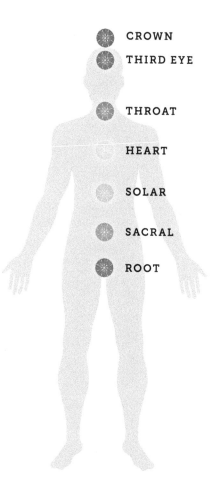

CROWN

THIRD EYE

THROAT

HEART

SOLAR

SACRAL

ROOT

# THE CHAKRA CENTERS

| Chakra Center | Color | Location | Body areas | Qualities | Affirmation |
|---|---|---|---|---|---|
| Root | Red | Base of the spine near the pelvis | Bones, small intestine, feet, blood | Strength, vitality, stability, grounding | I am grounded in present-moment consciousness and open to the universal flow. |
| Sacral | Orange | Between the pubic bone and the navel | Spleen, bladder, ovaries, testes, kidneys | Creativity, sexual energy, emotional balance | I allow the energy of my emotions to flow through me. |
| Solar Plexus | Yellow | In the hollow area below the sternum in the center of the stomach | Stomach, pancreas, large intestine | Confidence, courage, willpower, mental clarity | I am in touch with my inner power. |
| Heart | Green and pink | In the center of the chest | Heart, thymus, arms, hands | Balance, love, compassion, harmony | I am heart-centered and feel compassion and love flow through me. |
| Throat | Light blue | Base of the neck over the throat | Throat, neck, esophagus, thyroid, metabolism | Communication, truth, inner peace, self-expression | I express myself creatively, shining my inner light. |
| Third Eye | Indigo | Between and just above the eyes | Eyes, pineal gland, ears, nose | Intuition, psychic awareness | I am guided by my intuition. |
| Crown | Violet | Top of the head | Brain, pituitary gland, central nervous system | Connection, spirituality, personal transformation, oneness | I am a spiritual being and am one with all that is. |

## Choosing Crystals for Chakra Work

Although crystals are most commonly chosen by color for chakra balancing, stones may also be chosen for their associated properties. For example, if choosing a stone for inner strength for the solar plexus, you may select a stone like hematite, which is associated with strength, even though it is not yellow, the color associated with the solar plexus. You may also listen to your inner guidance and intuitively choose a stone to help realign the chakra center.

**Hematite is associated with strength.**

# Crystalline Meditations

Meditation is the art of stilling the mind until a place of inner peace has been attained. Within this stillness, you can connect with your true essence, your innermost self. You can explore the realms of consciousness and reflect on who you are as a spiritual being. Profound awakening can occur during meditation; it can be a powerful source of positive energy and transformation. Meditating as part of your daily routine allows you to bring balance to your body, mind, and spirit.

 **Finding time to meditate with your crystals can deepen your conscious awareness and enhance your connection with your spirit.**

When you introduce crystals into your meditation practice, they act as a point of focus, helping to raise your energetic vibration and promote mental clarity and conscious awareness. Meditating with your crystals also allows you to tune into their energy and receive intuitive insight about their uses and associated properties.

## Creating a Successful Meditation Practice

Meditation can seem intimidating if it's not something you're used to, but it doesn't have to be an intensely structured practice. There are no rules about how you must meditate, so you can do what works best for you. There are, however, a few things that can help getting into a meditation routine much simpler. You'll find various crystal meditations in the Crystal Sourcebook. For each of these meditations, follow the guidelines below to ensure success.

## Choose the Right Environment

Meditating within your sacred space will help to keep you safe and protected as well as spiritually supported during your session. Your environment has a great influence on your meditative experience, so be sure to meditate in a generally quiet place where you will not be disturbed. Your sacred space may also prove helpful by surrounding you with familiar high-vibrational objects to help raise your own frequency. Always be sure cleanse your space, and your crystals, before beginning your meditation.

## Meditation Routines

Creating a meditation routine can greatly enhance your ability to connect with your crystals and reach a place of stillness. Lighting candles or incense, sitting on your meditation cushion in front of your altar, playing soft music, and picking up your favorite crystal can all help create a ritual to alert your brain to the fact that you'll be entering a meditative state.

## Comfort is Key

You don't have to sit in the lotus position for hours on end to consider your meditation a success—in fact, this is more likely to hinder your progress. The most important thing in terms of posture is that you're comfortable. If your body isn't comfortable, you'll be distracted and focused on your body rather than on your mind. You can choose to sit, stand, or even lie down when you meditate as long as you are comfortable and able to maintain focus on the present moment.

## Breathe In . . . Breathe Out

Focusing on the breath is one of the oldest and most widely used meditation techniques. Practicing slow, even breathing allows your body to relax so that you can avoid physical distractions. It helps you to remove any mental clutter that may otherwise draw your attention away from present-moment consciousness. If, while meditating, you suddenly realize that your thoughts have wandered from the present, simply re-center yourself by focusing on your breathing.

## Releasing Expectations

Although all of these tips can help lead to a successful meditation practice, the most important thing is to release expectations of what your practice should be. Don't become attached to expected outcomes from your practice. Instead, allow yourself to just experience the energy of your stones and find inner stillness, without judgment or labels. Trust that whatever you experience is what's right for you at this moment and that your practice will grow and change over time.

 When meditating, it is important to find a relaxing location and to sit in a comfortable position.

# Crystal Sourcebook

*This sourcebook will show you which crystals to use for emotional healing and balance, spiritual healing and guidance, and shielding and protection from negativity. Using stones from these three important areas will help bring balance and healing to your body, mind, and spirit. Consult these pages with an open heart and mind and allow your intuition to guide you to the stones that are most needed by you at this time. Most of the crystals listed are commonly available, but some may be harder to come by. You will find a few suggested ways of working with each stone in this section. These techniques are simple and were designed to help to build your confidence. Crystal blessings for your journey!*

# Crystals for Emotional Healing

Like it or not, your emotions have the capability to influence everything you do. From the way you think about yourself and the world around you to the actions you take and the behaviors you exhibit, you are an emotional creature, ruled by more than logic alone.

Some emotions pass you by without much thought, but other emotional experiences make deep and lasting impressions on you. These are part of the human experience, but rather than allowing them to have a negative impact on your emotional and energetic well-being, you can learn to use crystal energy to cleanse them from your energy field and transmute them into positivity.

The following stones are known for their ability to do just this—heal emotional wounds and trauma and clear emotional debris from your aura. If you have some emotional healing work to do, no matter how big or how small, try working with one or more of the stones in this section.

# Agate (Blue Lace)

APPEARANCE/COLOR: Banded, pale blue with white "lace"
CURRENT AVAILABILITY: Widely available
PHYSIOLOGICAL CORRESPONDENCE: Thyroid, throat
PSYCHOLOGICAL CORRESPONDENCE: Forgiveness, empathy
KEYWORDS: Angelite, blue chalcedony, blue quartz, celestite
KEYWORDS: Communication, acceptance, emotional balance

## The Crystal

Blue lace agate is a translucent to opaque, massive mineral. It is easily identified by its layers of pale cornflower blue alternating with layers of white "lace." Blue lace agate is a banded form of chalcedony. Because this is a cryptocrystalline stone, it displays no outward crystal structure, but it belongs to the trigonal crystal system. Even though this stone is readily available, it is only found in parts of Kenya and Namibia.

## Attributes and Powers

Blue lace agate is a stone of forgiveness, helping you accept what has happened so you can release it. It encourages you to heal your emotions and find balance. Blue lace agate allows you to feel empathy and compassion for the person requiring your forgiveness and ensures that any energetic attachments are healed. It is a stone of positive communication, promoting assertiveness and personal power.

## Legendary Uses

This stone was discovered in the 1950s by George Swanson, a farmer in what is now named Namibia. It has developed a reputation in modern times as the "stone of ecology." In 1972, Mr. Swanson was moved by the words of American astronaut Dr. Harrison Schmitt, the only geologist to walk on the surface of the moon, when he said: "If ever there was a fragile-appearing piece of blue in space, it's the earth right now." Mr. Swanson knew that these stones could be a symbol of this "fragile blue." Blue lace agate was even, for a time, adopted as a symbol of earth ecology by the Tyler Ecology Award.

### HOW TO USE

Close your eyes and hold the stone in your hands while focusing on the person requiring your forgiveness. Allow yourself to feel any emotions surrounding the situation, listen to your inner truth about what has happened, and then let go of any unresolved feelings or negativity.

# Amazonite

APPEARANCE/COLOR: Opaque, pale blue-green to deep teal
CURRENT AVAILABILITY: Widely available
PHYSIOLOGICAL CORRESPONDENCE: Thymus, teeth, muscles
PSYCHOLOGICAL CORRESPONDENCE: Emotional balance, compassion, antianxiety
KEYWORDS: Emerald, turquoise, chrysocolla, quantum quattro silica
KEYWORDS: Nurturing, strength, inner peace, calm

## The Crystal

Amazonite is an opaque stone ranging from pale blue-green to deep teal, often with white to off-white streaks or speckles. Amazonite forms large, stubby, triclinic crystals that are typically found in clusters. It is a variety of microcline feldspar and typically grows alongside quartz and other silicate minerals. This mineral can be found all over the world, but some of the finest specimens come from Colorado, USA.

## Legendary Uses

Amazonite is named after the Amazon River, and some legends claim it was used by the Amazonians, a mythical tribe of warrior women. The stone was also used in ancient Egypt, where it was carved into tablets for part of the Book of the Dead. An amazonite scarab ring was found in Pharaoh Tutankhamun's tomb.

## Attributes and Powers

Amazonite is strongly connected to the thymus and the zeal point chakra, also known as the higher heart chakra or the seat of the soul. The zeal point is linked to your sense of inner peace and overall well-being. Amazonite has the ability to calm the emotions, especially anxiety and fear. You can use it to keep you calm in times of stress. It makes an excellent touchstone for strength and provides a sense of nurturing support when needed most.

### HOW TO USE

If you're feeling stressed or anxious, place an amazonite stone over your higher heart chakra, located about halfway between your heart and throat chakras. Take a deep, cleansing breath and slowly exhale. On your next inhalation, feel the soothing amazonite energy enter your body, calming you physically and emotionally. Slowly exhale. Repeat for at least two more breaths, or until you feel at ease.

# Apophyllite (Green)

**APPEARANCE/COLOR:** Transparent to translucent mint green to grass green

**CURRENT AVAILABILITY:** Uncommon

**PHYSIOLOGICAL CORRESPONDENCE:** Heart, neck, spine

**PSYCHOLOGICAL CORRESPONDENCE:** Stress reduction, calms anxiety

**KEYWORDS:** Chrysoprase, peridot, variscite

**KEYWORDS:** Reiki energy, distance healing, fairies, nature connection, meditation

## The Crystal

Green apophyllite is a transparent to translucent mineral that typically forms exquisite clusters of large, pyramid-shaped, mint-green crystal points. The stone is part of the zeolite group of minerals and is found in India and Canada. It displays a tetragonal crystal structure and its color derives from inclusions of celadonite. The more concentrated the celadonite, the deeper the green color of the mineral.

## Legendary Uses

Because of its recent discovery, this stone has no known legendary uses.

## Attributes and Powers

Green apophyllite is a stone of deep emotional healing. Its energy helps to lighten your heart. This crystal is known for attracting fairies and other nature spirits, encouraging you to be more playful and release stress or pressure directed at you from outside influences. Its connection with earth energy acts to calm anxiety and reduce worry. Green apophyllite is a stone of abundance and removes concern or anxiety over financial issues, allowing you to trust in the universe's ability to provide for you.

### HOW TO USE

Add a small crystal or cluster to a houseplant to encourage the presence of fairies and nature spirits in your home or sacred space. Green apophyllite is excellent used in the center of a crystal grid for sending distance-healing energy to others. Place a green apophyllite crystal in a place of prominence in your home to attract more abundance into your life. Remember, this is not just financial abundance, but rather an abundance of all that you need to support you. Be sure to sit with this crystal often and make a mental list of all that you would like to draw into your life.

# Aquamarine

**APPEARANCE/COLOR:** Transparent to translucent light blue to blue-green
**CURRENT AVAILABILITY:** Widely available
**PHYSIOLOGICAL CORRESPONDENCE:** Circulatory system, cellular regeneration
**PSYCHOLOGICAL CORRESPONDENCE:** Acceptance, forgiveness, calm
**KEYWORDS:** Celestite, blue topaz, aqua aura quartz
**KEYWORDS:** Emotional cleansing, peace, tranquillity, angelic communication

## The Crystal

Aquamarine is a blue to blue-green variety of beryl. It displays a hexagonal crystal system and may be transparent to translucent. It is found in many locations across the globe, but some of the best specimens come from Brazil, Pakistan, and Namibia. This mineral is often heat-treated to intensify its color.

## Attributes and Powers

Aquamarine is immensely calming and can reduce anxiety better than almost any other healing stone (especially when paired with lepidolite). The light-blue color corresponds to the throat chakra, so the stone's energy can facilitate communication with your angels and guides. Use this stone to help you release attachments and "go with the flow" during difficult situations.

## Legendary Uses

Aquamarine is the March birthstone. There is a legend about the origins of this gem that claims the stone came from a mermaid's jewelry box. Its name is derived from the Latin words for "sea water." It has an extensive history of use across the globe.

### HOW TO USE

Hold a piece of aquamarine in your hands, make yourself comfortable, and close your eyes. Take a deep breath in, inhaling the energy of the stone deep into your body. Let its energy wash over you in a wave of calm. Feel its energy pass through your aura like cleansing ripples of sea water, cleansing your field with the ebb and flow of crystal energy. Focus on the stone in your hands and visualize a blue light begin to pool there. See this light expand outward from your hands, filling your entire body with the gentle energy of the aquamarine stone.

# Calcite (Aqua)

APPEARANCE/COLOR: Translucent aqua, blue-green

CURRENT AVAILABILITY: Very common

PHYSIOLOGICAL CORRESPONDENCE: Skeletal system, teeth, thymus gland

PSYCHOLOGICAL CORRESPONDENCE: Compassion, calmness, self-care

KEYWORDS: Blue opal, gem silica, green aventurine

KEYWORDS: Heart healing, emotional purging, healthy habits, soul connection

## The Crystal

Aqua calcite is typically found in massive form in both Mexico and Argentina and displays a mild blue to sea-green color. Calcite is a member of the trigonal crystal system. Although widely available, the blue-green color of this calcite is less common than other colors. The rough stones are often treated with a weak acid wash to take off any rough edges, giving them a waxy feel.

## Legendary Uses

There are no known historic uses of this stone, though some modern crystal healers do believe it has connections to the mythological continent of Atlantis.

## Attributes and Powers

Aqua calcite is a gentle, yet powerful, stone. It encourages healthy eating habits and helps you to develop positive self-care routines. It contains the energy of the sea on a calm day. A stone for heart healing, aqua calcite repairs trauma and allows you to feel compassion for yourself while you heal. It purges negative emotions or ones that keep you trapped in cycles of self-neglect. Aqua calcite is a high vibrational emotional healer and helps you discover that everything in this world can be healed with love. This crystal helps you to develop positive soul-level connections between yourself and others.

### HOW TO USE

Fill a large bowl with water. Make yourself comfortable and drop your aqua calcite stone gently into the center of the bowl. Focus your gaze on the ripples on the water's surface. Allow your eyes to soften, going in and out of focus, and hold your gaze on the ripples. Watch the water as it slowly and gently returns to a calm, still state and feel your inner emotions harmonize with that of the calm water. Remove the stone from the water, dry it gently with a soft cloth and hold it to your heart chakra. Close your eyes and visualize the ripples of your heart, your emotional center, slowing to a calm, still state. Remain in silent meditation for as long as you like, feeling the gentle energy of the aqua calcite stone.

# Calcite (Pink Cobalto)

APPEARANCE/COLOR: Translucent to transparent rose pink to magenta
CURRENT AVAILABILITY: Available from most specialty stores
PHYSIOLOGICAL CORRESPONDENCE: Metabolism, immune system, colon
PSYCHOLOGICAL CORRESPONDENCE: Passion, excitement, motivation
KEYWORDS: Ruby aura quartz, pink spinel, pink tourmaline
KEYWORDS: Romance, love, vitality, magic

## The Crystal

This exquisite variety of calcite ranges from soft rose pink to deep magenta in color. It occasionally displays trigonal crystals, but it is more commonly seen as a crystal druze atop a matrix. Some of the best pieces come from Morocco, but this mineral is also found in the Democratic Republic of Congo, Australia, and Spain.

## Legendary Uses

This stone has no known legendary or historical uses.

## Attributes and Powers

Cobalto calcite's deep magenta color is a natural vitality magnet. Use this crystal to energize and motivate you, especially to pursue the things that you're most passionate about. This crystal can add a spark to your romantic life in relationships where the flames of passion seem to be dwindling. This stone can rekindle your connection to your partner and promotes unconditional love. It is a magical stone and can be a great source of support during times of personal growth, transformation, and new beginnings.

### HOW TO USE

To rekindle passion and romance in your relationship, place this crystal on a desk or table and take time to sit down and start a journal about yourself and your partner. What do you love most about him or her and about your relationship together? Which aspects of your relationship require healing or forgiveness to move forward? How can you establish trust and vulnerability with one another? What is missing from your relationship that you wish you had? Once you have a list, hold your crystal in your hands and speak these things aloud to manifest them into being for the highest good of you and your partner.

# Calcite (Pink Mangano)

**APPEARANCE/COLOR:** Opaque banded pink and white or transparent pale pink
**CURRENT AVAILABILITY:** Fairly common
**PHYSIOLOGICAL CORRESPONDENCE:** Muscle tissue, tongue, reproductive organs
**PSYCHOLOGICAL CORRESPONDENCE:** Compassion, empathy, emotional healing
**KEYWORDS:** Pink opal, morganite, rose quartz
**KEYWORDS:** Connection, friendship, independence

## The Crystal

This trigonal crystal is a pale pink variety of calcite. It is commonly opaque and banded with layers of pale pink and creamy white. The best pieces of this type can be found in Peru. The stone also forms small crystal clusters or crystal druze in a soft pink color. Some of the highest quality crystals and clusters are from China.

## Legendary Uses

This stone has no known legendary or historical uses.

## Attributes and Powers

Pink mangano calcite promotes genuine emotional connection between you and your friends or loved ones. It's an excellent stone for healers who want to connect to their clients in a deeper way to better understand their needs during an energy-healing session. It facilitates a harmonizing of the energy between the healer and the client, enhancing the effectiveness of the session. It is particularly helpful for Reiki masters or massage therapists. It can also be used to facilitate new friendships or to encourage growth in existing friendships.

### HOW TO USE

Pink mangano calcite is best used to facilitate a deep connection with others. Begin by holding the crystal in your receiving hand (your nondominant hand) and inviting the other person to place their receiving hand on top of the stone, so that the crystal is held between each of you. Close your eyes and focus on tuning into the other person's energy field, understanding them physically, emotionally, mentally, and spiritually. Feel yourself connect to the other person so that you're attuned to their energy field and know how best to serve them.

# Chrysocolla

**APPEARANCE/COLOR:** Generally opaque; ranges from bright blue to turquoise-green
**CURRENT AVAILABILITY:** Common
**PHYSIOLOGICAL CORRESPONDENCE:** Cardiovascular system, heart, veins
**PSYCHOLOGICAL CORRESPONDENCE:** Forgiveness, joy, peace
**KEYWORDS:** Turquoise, quantum quattro silica, blue opal
**KEYWORDS:** Inspiration, care and concern for others, ecological awareness

## The Crystal

This secondary, copper-based mineral is part of the orthorhombic crystal system. It ranges in color from robin's egg blue to teal green and is most commonly seen as botryoidal clusters. It is commonly found in the Democratic Republic of Congo, Peru, China, and Arizona. Although almost always opaque, very high quality crystalline pieces may be transparent to translucent.

## Attributes and Powers

Chrysocolla can be used for earth healing and to promote ecological awareness and care and concern for Mother Earth and all of her creatures. This is a stone of environmental champions and pioneers. Just as this crystal can be used to rid the earth of toxins and debris, it can do the same for your emotional body. It is a powerful cleanser and auric healer.

## Legendary Uses

Chrysocolla was first named by Theophrastus in the year 315 BCE. There are tales linking the stone to the legendary mines of King Solomon; it is said that God told Solomon that the stone captured the likeness of the view of earth from heaven above. Chrysocolla was revered in ancient Egypt where it was seen as a wisdom stone by the likes of Cleopatra and Nefertiti and was carried by each of them in order to provide guidance in rulership. This mineral is also said to have been used by Apache peoples for healing.

### HOW TO USE

Go to your favorite spot in nature with your chrysocolla stone. Make yourself comfortable and place the stone on the ground. Hold your hands over the crystal, close your eyes, and tune into the stone's energy. Visualize green, healing light surrounding the chrysocolla. See the light grow and expand out from the stone until it's quite large. Use your hands to push the ball of light toward the earth's center. Visualize the light traveling through the earth until it reaches the core. See the light expand, healing the earth as it passes through every layer, every particle of soil, every plant and animal.

# Danburite (Pink)

APPEARANCE/COLOR: Transparent to translucent; extremely pale pink color
CURRENT AVAILABILITY: Available from most specialty crystal stores
PHYSIOLOGICAL CORRESPONDENCE: Neurological system, heart
PSYCHOLOGICAL CORRESPONDENCE: Overcoming grief, emotional healing after trauma
KEYWORDS: Morganite, pink petalite, rose quartz
KEYWORDS: Healing emotional wounds, inner-child work, cheerfulness

## The Crystal

Pink danburite is a transparent to translucent variety of danburite that typically forms large solitary crystal points with a very pale pink color, although it is sometimes also found in small clusters. It is a silicate mineral that displays an orthorhombic crystal structure. Danburite was originally discovered in Danbury, Connecticut, but the highest quality pink pieces are found in Mexico.

## Legendary Uses

Danburite is relatively new to the crystal market— it was only discovered in the late nineteenth century. It does not have any known historical uses or associated lore.

## Attributes and Powers

Pink danburite has an incredibly soft, gentle energy and is a perfect healing stone to use with those who have suffered from any type of abuse or trauma, physical or emotional. It provides energetic support so that you feel nurtured and cared for, allowing you to heal old wounds. It is a stone of acceptance and forgiveness and encourages you to move forward after tragedy or grief. Pink danburite can help to open your heart chakra if it has shut down due to hurt or neglect. This stone is known for soothing children in need of healing.

### HOW TO USE

Place a piece of pink danburite over your sacral chakra to balance your emotions, or over your heart chakra to promote self-love, forgiveness, and acceptance. Keep the crystal in place for approximately 10 minutes or until you intuitively feel that the energy has shifted. If the source of your grief or trauma causes you to lie awake at night, unable to sleep, you may place this crystal in your pillowcase or on your bedside table to promote feelings of safety and security.

# Dioptase

APPEARANCE/COLOR: Transparent; deep emerald green
CURRENT AVAILABILITY: Widely available, but high-quality pieces can be costly
PHYSIOLOGICAL CORRESPONDENCE: Regulation of blood pressure, thymus
PSYCHOLOGICAL CORRESPONDENCE: Compassion, mercy, empathy
KEYWORDS: Emerald, malachite, bloodstone, green aventurine
KEYWORDS: Heart healing, forgiveness, consciousness expansion, dissolution of ego

## The Crystal

Dioptase is a trigonal crystal of deep green color. It most commonly forms exquisitely transparent crystal clusters. It was thought that the best quality pieces came from Kazakhstan until the more recent discovery of a magnificent pocket of dioptase in Namibia.

## Legendary Uses

Dioptase was named in 1797 from the Greek words **dia**, for "through," and **optomao**, "to see," describing the gem's transparency. It has a long history of being mistaken for the more valuable emerald of similar color.

## Attributes and Powers

This gem promotes compassion and kindness like no other. It connects to the energy of the goddess Kwan Yin, whose tears of mercy are poured down to any who are suffering here on earth rather than reaching enlightenment. This crystal can help you to see your inner beauty and encourages self-love. If you have trouble making time to take care of yourself, this crystal can help you develop a positive, healing, self-care routine. This stone is an excellent companion if you feel as though you're "not good enough" or that you are "not deserving" of the good things in your life. It can help you to overcome fear-based thoughts that dwell in the ego mind in order to replace them with a more positive mindset.

### HOW TO USE

Hold dioptase over your heart chakra in times of despair and ask for the assistance of your guides, angels, or Ascended Masters with what troubles you. Keep the stone with you, in your pocket or purse, to help keep the energy of these helpful beings nearby.

# Eudialyte

APPEARANCE/COLOR: Opaque to translucent; blush bronze-pink to deep magenta
CURRENT AVAILABILITY: Rare
PHYSIOLOGICAL CORRESPONDENCE: Thyroid, heart, liver
PSYCHOLOGICAL CORRESPONDENCE: Bravery, courage, forgiveness
KEYWORDS: Rubellite tourmaline, red spinel, ruby
KEYWORDS: Strength, vitality, selflessness, generosity

## The Crystal

Eudialyte is a trigonal crystal that is typically found as massive, deep magenta stones. It can also be found as bronze-pink to rose-pink crystals on a matrix, but these crystals are rare. The massive stones are more readily available than crystals, but may still be difficult to come by. The best quality rough stones come from Canada, Greenland, or Russia and display a deep magenta color.

## Legendary Uses

There is a legend among the Saami people of Scandinavia that describes their battle with an enemy. It is said that the battle caused great bloodshed and that eudialyte is the blood of the Saami people turned to stone to commemorate the battle.

## Attributes and Powers

Eudialyte promotes generosity and selfless acts and is an excellent companion stone for charitable pursuits of any kind. It can ease tension during an argument and is known for cooling tempers so that logic rather than emotion can prevail in a disagreement. Eudialyte can be used to give you strength during difficult times. It also promotes vitality and increases your energy levels so that you can complete even the most exhausting task.

### HOW TO USE

If you know that you must have a difficult discussion with someone, or if a disagreement is imminent, reach for your eudialyte crystal to help you keep a level head. Ask the crystal to help keep you calm and to guide your words and body language to remain cool and collected. Hold the intention to remain emotionally neutral and feel your energy body become balanced by soothing vibrations of the eudialyte stone.

# Hiddenite

**APPEARANCE/COLOR:** Transparent yellow-green to pale mint green
**CURRENT AVAILABILITY:** Limited availability
**PHYSIOLOGICAL CORRESPONDENCE:** Sinuses, digestive system
**PSYCHOLOGICAL CORRESPONDENCE:** Inquisitiveness, psychic exploration
**KEYWORDS:** Green apophyllite, tsavorite garnet, prehnite
**KEYWORDS:** Magic, revealing secrets, mystery, mysticism, herbalism

## The Crystal

Hiddenite is the rare, green variety of spodumene. It is a monoclinic crystal displaying striations on the surface of pale green transparent crystals. This mineral is often artificially irradiated to intensify its color (especially in specimens originating from Afghanistan and Pakistan).

## Legendary Uses

This mineral was named in 1879 for its discoverer, American mineralogist William E. Hidden, and due to its somewhat recent discovery, it has no known historical uses.

## Attributes and Powers

Hiddenite is a gentle heart healer. It exposes truths about that which is being hidden from you in important areas of your life, but only if it is for your highest good to learn that what is revealed. Hiddenite encourages journey work and psychic exploration and is especially helpful for communicating with plant spirits. It assists in the study of herbalism and natural medicines. Hiddenite also encourages you to seek out mystical experiences that may have deep and profound meaning for your life's journey.

### HOW TO USE

Keep a piece of hiddenite on your desk or table if studying any type of natural or holistic medicine to assist you in fully absorbing the information. Additionally, you can place a piece of hiddenite in your herb garden to promote healthy plant growth. To reveal deceitful people, or things that are being hidden from you, hold a hiddenite crystal over your third eye and take mental note of any words, messages, or symbols that come to you intuitively. Take a few moments to jot them down on a piece of paper, and then, while holding your hiddenite crystal in your receiving (nondominant) hand, try to decipher the message that is being presented to you.

# Kunzite

APPEARANCE/COLOR: Transparent lavender to pink
CURRENT AVAILABILITY: Somewhat limited availability
PHYSIOLOGICAL CORRESPONDENCE: Heart, feet, hands, joints
PSYCHOLOGICAL CORRESPONDENCE: Bliss, contentment
KEYWORDS: Rose quartz, pink halite, morganite
KEYWORDS: Nonattachment, positivity, faith

## The Crystal

Kunzite is the semi-rare, pink variety of spodumene. It is a monoclinic crystal displaying striations on the surface of lavender pink, transparent crystals. This mineral is often artificially irradiated to intensify its color (especially in specimens originating from Afghanistan and Pakistan).

## Legendary Uses

This mineral was named in 1903 in honor of American mineralogist George Frederick Kunz. Because of its relatively recent discovery, kunzite has no known historical significance.

## Attributes and Powers

Kunzite is a very gentle stone. For people who are highly sensitive to crystal energy, it is an excellent crystal with which to work. Kunzite promotes bliss and absolute positivity of mind. It acts to push negative patterns out of your energy field by filling you up with high vibrational energy. It is a stone of the higher heart chakra, working to help you manifest peace and contentment into all facets of your life. This stone can also help to reaffirm your faith in the universe/god/goddess/spirit after trying times. It has a soft, healing vibration that can also help reduce anxiety, in people and in animals. This crystal encourages you to be playful and allow yourself to take necessary breaks from work or pressing responsibilities when it would prove beneficial to your health and mental well-being.

### HOW TO USE

Keep a piece of kunzite on your person during difficult life periods or major changes (i.e. moving, divorce, career change, retirement, etc.) to help smooth the transition and help you maintain a positive outlook. It is best worn as a pendant over the heart chakra, but may also be carried in your pocket or purse.

# Larimar

**APPEARANCE/COLOR:** Opaque, light blue with white or green swirls

**CURRENT AVAILABILITY:** Rare, but available in most specialty stores

**PHYSIOLOGICAL CORRESPONDENCE:** Thyroid gland, thymus gland, throat, vocal cords

**PSYCHOLOGICAL CORRESPONDENCE:** Mental clarity, expanded consciousness

**KEYWORDS:** Blue opal, celestite, aquamarine, blue calcite

**KEYWORDS:** Inner-child work, animal communication, oneness, connection

## The Crystal

Larimar is a rare, blue variety of pectolite found only in the Dominican Republic. The blue color of this stone, often mottled with white or green, resembles the ocean when glistening with sunlight. Lower-quality pieces will sometimes contain red or brown flecks. High-quality larimar sometimes displays a slight pearlescence. Although massive in its outward appearance, this mineral is part of the triclinic crystal system.

## Legendary Uses

Although originally discovered in 1916, it wasn't until the stone's rediscovery in 1974 that it found popularity in the market. Because of its recent introduction, it does not have any known historical uses.

## Attributes and Powers

Larimar is a gentle stone of deep and profound healing. It is sometimes known as the "dolphin stone" and has a strong connection to communication. It is thought to facilitate communication between people, especially about difficult situations, with animals, or with spirit guides. It is also linked to the water element and is used for expanding conscious awareness. A stone of empathy and compassion, it helps you tap into feelings of oneness with all beings in the universe, promoting feelings of belonging to the whole.

### HOW TO USE

Larimar is best used in a medicine pouch or worn as jewelry. However, you can also hold a larimar stone over your throat chakra to enhance positive communication. Alternatively, try placing a piece of larimar near each of your ears to enhance your ability to hear important messages from totem animals or spirit guides.

# Lepidolite

APPEARANCE/COLOR: Opaque; pearlescent pink to lavender

CURRENT AVAILABILITY: Uncommon, but available from most specialty stores

PHYSIOLOGICAL CORRESPONDENCE: Brain, lungs, blood cells, spine, neck

PSYCHOLOGICAL CORRESPONDENCE: PTSD, bipolar disorder, depression

KEYWORDS: Amethyst, spirit quartz, lavender fluorite

KEYWORDS: Balance, emotional well-being, peace, intellect

## The Crystal

Lepidolite is a monoclinic, lithium-rich form of mica. It is typically opaque, but very high-quality pieces can be translucent. It ranges from sparkly lavender to a shimmering, pearlescent pink or lilac color. Stunning lavender lepidolite can be found in California, deep purple lepidolite in Mexico, and gemmy lilac lepidolite in Brazil. It is sometimes also referred to as lavenderine.

## Legendary Uses

This crystal was named for the Greek words **lepidos**, for "scale," and **lithos**, for "stone," in 1792. This stone has no known historical use.

## Attributes and Powers

Lepidolite is one of the absolute best stones for helping to reduce anxiety and stress (or even PTSD), especially when combined with the soothing energy of aquamarine. It balances the hemispheres of the brain, bringing balance and emotional well-being. It also aids in healing the lungs and disorders affecting the blood cells (especially those affecting oxygen levels in the blood). Because of its high lithium content, lepidolite is a useful energetic support for those suffering from bipolar disorder, or depression. When paired with pink tourmaline, it makes a powerful energetic shield, protecting you from negativity by transmuting lower vibrations into love energy.

## HOW TO USE

Wear lepidolite as a pair of bracelets (one on each wrist) or earrings to balance the hemispheres of the brain and bring balance and stability to your physical, mental, and emotional bodies. Lepidolite makes the perfect companion for times when you're feeling anxious. Carry a small tumbled stone in your pocket during times of great stress or worry to reduce the discomfort and fear that often accompany anxiety.

# Okenite

**APPEARANCE/COLOR:** Opaque, white to off-white
**CURRENT AVAILABILITY:** Somewhat common
**PHYSIOLOGICAL CORRESPONDENCE:** Cartilage, hair, teeth, nails
**PSYCHOLOGICAL CORRESPONDENCE:** Understanding, forgiveness
**KEYWORDS:** Selenite, scolecite, howlite, white onyx
**KEYWORDS:** Emotional release, cooperation, gentleness, fragility, flexibility

## The Crystal

Okenite is a triclinic mineral found in spherical clusters of opaque white to off-white needles. These spherical clusters looks like cotton balls or snowballs and are typically found within basalt geodes. This mineral appears "fuzzy" and its tiny crystals will bend (or break) when touched. Okenite is found in many locations, but the highest quality pieces come from areas near Mumbai, India.

and facilitates the emotional release that often accompanies this process. Okenite has a gentle energy and is symbolic of the fragility of the emotional body. It does, however, encourage you to be flexible in your attitudes and behaviors so that you can go with the flow of life rather than being rigid and in opposition to change.

## Legendary Uses

This mineral was officially named in 1828 after biologist Lorenz Oken. It has no known legendary uses.

## Attributes and Powers

Okenite is an extremely soft stone, both physically and energetically. It promotes mutual understanding and cooperation between people. It also aids in forgiveness

### HOW TO USE

Set this crystal in a place of prominence where you will see it often. Use it as a symbol or reminder to be flexible in your life. It's healthier to be flexible and bend and sway as needed than to be rigid and break or snap against the winds of change. You may even choose to place this stone on your altar or in your sacred space and use it as a point of focus in meditation. Additionally, okenite can be placed in your kitchen or living room to promote mutual understanding among family members, or in your office or conference room to encourage coworkers to work cooperatively.

# Opal (Blue)

APPEARANCE/COLOR: Translucent to opaque robin's egg blue
CURRENT AVAILABILITY: Limited availability; rare
PHYSIOLOGICAL CORRESPONDENCE: Thymus, tear ducts, eyes
PSYCHOLOGICAL CORRESPONDENCE: Emotional release, prioritization
KEYWORDS: Blue apatite, blue opal, blue smithsonite, gem silica
KEYWORDS: Earth energy, Gaia consciousness, nurturing, heart healing, discernment

## The Crystal

An amorphous mineral with no internal crystalline structure, blue opal is a hydrated form of silica. This blue variety of opal gets its color from inclusions of chrysocolla and is sometimes known as chrysopal. It is also referred to as "Andes opal" or "Andean opal" because it is only found near the Andes Mountains in Peru. Blue opal is a common opal and does not display the play of color that can be seen in precious opals. This stone is frequently dyed to enhance its color, so buy it from a reputable source to ensure its authenticity.

## Attributes and Powers

Blue opal is a powerful healing stone. It allows you to tap into the energy of the earth to recharge and rejuvenate yourself. It assists you in seeing emotional patterns that need to be released as well as supporting you during the release itself. This crystal helps you see that there is an abundance of happiness and joy waiting for you, and facilitates the shedding of happy tears rather than sad ones.

## Legendary Uses

Blue opal was used for protection and healing by the people of Peru. The Incas believed this opal to be a gift from Pachamama, the goddess of earth energy and abundance. It was also believed by the Aztecs and the Incas to be the eyes of the gods, left here on earth. It is now the national stone of Peru.

### HOW TO USE

Place this stone over your heart or third eye while out in nature. Breathe deep and feel your connection to Gaia and all living beings. Know that you are nurtured and supported on your life's journey.

# Petalite

**APPEARANCE/COLOR:** Transparent clear to very pale pink
**CURRENT AVAILABILITY:** Fairly common, but difficult to obtain
**PHYSIOLOGICAL CORRESPONDENCE:** Pituitary gland, pineal gland, brain
**PSYCHOLOGICAL CORRESPONDENCE:** Mental clarity, emotional stability, objectivity
**KEYWORDS:** Ulexite, scolecite, clear quartz
**KEYWORDS:** Psychic awareness, expanded consciousness, connection

## The Crystal

Petalite is a glassy-looking monoclinic mineral that typically forms massive deposits. It rarely forms crystals. It is most commonly colorless, but may have a slight pink tinge.

## Legendary Uses

This stone has no known historical significance.

## Attributes and Powers

Petalite is a very high vibrational crystal.
It is strongly linked with the angelic realm and can be used to facilitate a connection with your guides and angels. When you need deep emotional healing, petalite can be used to receive support and energetic healing from your angels. It also encourages you to trust your intuition and inner sight. It can strengthen the energy of your pineal gland and enhance psychic awareness, opening you up to the messages that surround you.

### HOW TO USE

To heal deep emotional wounds, hold a piece of petalite in your hands or place one over your heart chakra. Close your eyes and take a deep, cleansing breath. Visualize the stone glowing very bright, like a beacon for your guides and angels. Invite your guides and angels into the space and see them slowly begin to surround you. Think about the emotional aspects of yourself that require deep healing and request that your guides assist you by restoring you to balanced wholeness and a state of perfect emotional well-being. Send your gratitude and love to your guides for their assistance by visualizing the bright light from your petalite moving into the heart center of each of your guides and angels, giving them the gift of sacred crystal energy. Take another deep, cleansing breath and open your eyes.

# Quartz (Celadonite)

APPEARANCE/COLOR: Mint green phantom within transparent clear crystal

CURRENT AVAILABILITY: Limited availability

PHYSIOLOGICAL CORRESPONDENCE: Endocrine glands, heart

PSYCHOLOGICAL CORRESPONDENCE: Playfulness, love

KEYWORDS: Green apophyllite, chlorite quartz, prehnite

KEYWORDS: Magic, nature spirits, inner-child healing

## The Crystal

Celadonite quartz is most often found in the form of small phantom points or clusters. Celadonite has a monoclinic crystal system and is part of the mica group while quartz is a silicate mineral with a hexagonal crystal system.

## Legendary Uses

These crystals are a fairly recent discovery from Madagascar so they have no known historical use. They have been trademarked under a different name (referring to the spirits or devas thought to live within these stones).

## Attributes and Powers

Celadonite quartz is a stone of happiness, joy, and love. It encourages you to be playful and appreciate the niceties of life. It is a beneficial stone for mothers and children and can even be used for inner-child healing. Celadonite quartz promotes the release of emotional baggage and trauma accumulated during childhood that has carried over into your life as an adult. This stone has also been said to attract fairies and other magical beings.

### HOW TO USE

Place a piece of celadonite quartz in your garden, or on your altar, to attract fairies or nature spirits. You can hold a crystal over your heart chakra to heal your inner child. While holding the stone, intend to release any hurt or trauma from your childhood that may be affecting your patterns of behavior in adulthood. You may even choose to ask for the assistance of fairies and other magical beings to protect and nurture your inner child while this work is carried out.

# Rhodochrosite

APPEARANCE/COLOR: Transparent magenta to opaque, pink and white bands
CURRENT AVAILABILITY: Common, but high-quality crystals are difficult to obtain
PHYSIOLOGICAL CORRESPONDENCE: Heart, muscles, tendons, lung tissue
PSYCHOLOGICAL CORRESPONDENCE: Compassion, empathy, forgiveness
KEYWORDS: Rhodonite, pink tourmaline, ruby
KEYWORDS: Honor, ancestral healing, karmic healing

## The Crystal

Rhodochrosite is a soft trigonal mineral with a variety of appearances. It can form translucent to transparent crystals ranging from magenta to red, as well as opaque swirling layers of pink and white lace. High-quality pieces can be found in Colorado in the USA, China, and Peru while the banded stalactites are from Argentina.

## Legendary Uses

The Incas believed this mineral was the crystallized blood of former Incan royalty and it is said to have been discovered by a ruler named Inca Ripac (also called Viracocha). Rhodochrosite was used to create Incan funerary jewelry. For this reason, it is sometimes known as Inca rose or rosinca. It is said that there is a large, sacred, heart-shaped rhodochrosite boulder deep beneath the Andes that "beats" once every two hundred years. It is the national stone of Argentina and the state mineral of Colorado.

## Attributes and Powers

Rhodochrosite can be used for clearing karma and negativity from your ancestral line. Its energy permeates your being, on a DNA level, to remove detrimental karmic patterning and trauma from your field. Use rhodochrosite to promote forgiveness and empathy stemming from trauma or emotional abuse, in this lifetime or from past lives. It energetically restores the soft tissues of the body after injury or illness.

### HOW TO USE

Place this stone in front of you, close your eyes, and drum in rhythm with your heartbeat. Visualize the sound of the drum amplifying the energy of the stone and feel the stone's energy surround you as you drum. Start drumming louder and feel yourself release any negativity or karmic patterning from your being. Slowly reduce the volume of your drumming until it is completely quiet. Take a deep breath in, exhale, and open your eyes.

# Tourmaline (Pink)

**APPEARANCE/COLOR:** Transparent; light pink to deep magenta
**CURRENT AVAILABILITY:** Limited availability
**PHYSIOLOGICAL CORRESPONDENCE:** Hands, skin, heart, intestines
**PSYCHOLOGICAL CORRESPONDENCE:** Personal growth, love
**KEYWORDS:** Rhodochrosite, pink spinel, red spinel
**KEYWORDS:** Emotional release, past-life healing, DNA healing

## The Crystal

Pink tourmaline is a trigonal crystal with sub-varieties including elbaite and rubellite. It forms striated crystals, typically in small clusters. It is found in many locations across the globe, but the highest quality pieces are from Brazil.

## Legendary Uses

Pink tourmaline is an alternative to opal for the October birthstone. It has been mistaken for ruby throughout history, and the red gems found within the Russian crown jewels are not ruby, as previously thought, but are actually deep pink tourmaline crystals. There is an Egyptian legend about how tourmaline acquired its variety of colors. The legend states that tourmaline journeyed along a rainbow as it moved from the center of the earth to try and get nearer to the sun. Along the way, the stone absorbed all of the colors of the rainbow.

## Attributes and Powers

Pink tourmaline is a stone of deep healing. It cleanses emotional debris on a DNA level. It is an excellent stone for past-life healing and cleansing negative patterning from your family line. It facilitates karmic cleansing through access to the Akashic Records. By helping you see your soul contracts and karmic patterns, you can choose to make changes on your soul's path.

### HOW TO USE

Hold a piece of pink tourmaline in your hands for a moment, tuning into its energy. Place it on your desk while you do some writing. Focus your intention on receiving messages from the Akashic Records about your soul's path and any karmic patterning that may be hindering your personal growth or spiritual evolution. Write down everything that comes to you—words, symbols, phrases, sketches of images—anything. Do this without judgement or censorship. When you feel ready, hold the stone in your hands as you review what you have written and try to decipher the messages. Think about what steps you can take going forward to release this negative patterning.

# Crystals for Spiritual Healing and Guidance

Do you think of yourself as intuitive? Believe it or not, all people have inherent intuitive capabilities, but over time, they lose touch with these natural psychic skills. Rather than accept their intuitive gifts, some people fight against this communication from the spirit.

Crystals can help you to hone your inner guidance in a way that's appropriate for you. They help to boost your confidence in your intuitive abilities as well as creating energetic boundaries to keep you safe and protected when opening up psychically.

Additionally, healing crystals can aid in reconnecting with the spiritual aspect of yourself. This enhanced connection can deepen meditation, help you learn to recognize present-moment awareness, and also communicate with your spirit guides and angels. These experiences can help you evolve both personally and spiritually, bringing you closer to your whole, perfect, spiritual self.

# Agate (Shiva's Eye)

APPEARANCE/COLOR: Opaque gray-blue with black and brown spots
CURRENT AVAILABILITY: Limited availability
PHYSIOLOGICAL CORRESPONDENCE: Pineal gland, eyes, brain
PSYCHOLOGICAL CORRESPONDENCE: Oneness
KEYWORDS: Sardonyx, banded agate, gray chrysoberyl
KEYWORDS: Intuition, psychic protection, connection

## The Crystal

Shiva's eye agates are natural "eye" agates from India. A variety of chalcedony, these opaque cryptocrystalline stones display a gray-blue background with brown to black spots. Sometimes the spots are even framed with a thin brown ring, giving the appearance of a pupil and iris. The stones are typically cut into an eye shape to accentuate their eyelike appearance.

## Legendary Uses

These crystals are associated with Lord Shiva, the Hindu god of meditation and spiritual pursuit. Shiva is one of the three main Hindu deities and is traditionally connected with yoga and the arts.

## Attributes and Powers

Shiva's eye agates are powerful stones for awakening your psychic gifts. They are known for their ability to open the third eye chakra in those who have been closed off from their intuitive abilities. The eye symbol also has a strong connection to spiritual and psychic protection and is known for warding off the "evil eye" and other negativity from external sources. This stone can help you tap into your innate psychic gifts, enhancing clairvoyance and clairaudience. It is a beneficial stone for mediums because of its ability to keep them protected while connecting with those who have crossed over.

### HOW TO USE

Hold the stone in your hands or place it on your third eye chakra. Close your physical eyes and visualize universal energy coming into the stone and moving into your body, filling your body with light. This light keeps you protected while awakening your psychic gifts. Clear your mind of all idle chatter and allow yourself to open up to the messages the universe wishes to send you. They may appear as words, symbols, or pictures, or you may hear them being spoken to you by your guides.

# Amethyst

**APPEARANCE/COLOR:** Transparent to translucent violet to deep purple

**CURRENT AVAILABILITY:** Common

**PHYSIOLOGICAL CORRESPONDENCE:** Liver, pancreas, chest

**PSYCHOLOGICAL CORRESPONDENCE:** Addiction, mental clarity, desire

**KEYWORDS:** Sugilite, charoite, stichitite

**KEYWORDS:** Spirituality, dreams, meditation, astral travel

## The Crystal

Amethyst is a purple macrocrystalline variety of quartz found throughout the globe. Amethyst crystals may display a trigonal or hexagonal crystal system.

These crystals may be found as large single points or as clusters of small points coating a matrix. Colors range from pale lilac, to bright violet, to deep purple.

## Legendary Uses

Amethyst has a long history of use as a healing stone. Its use by humans dates back to as early as 25,000 BCE. It is the February birthstone. Amethyst is said to have acquired its purple color from a cup of wine poured onto it by Bacchus, the Roman god of agriculture. It has long been viewed as a symbol of spirituality and can frequently be seen in rings adorning the fingers of bishops. There are several references to the amethyst stone in the Bible, including its mention as one of the twelve stones set in the breastplate of Aaron, the High Priest of Israel. The ancient Egyptians associated this stone with their zodiac symbol of the goat.

## Attributes and Powers

Amethyst is a great companion for deeply spiritual people, or for those who would like to rekindle their connection to the spiritual aspect of themselves. You can use amethyst to enhance meditation, dream work, astral travel, and journey work, or to deepen mystical experiences. Amethyst crystals work to activate the crown chakra, awakening your intuitive and spiritual gifts.

### HOW TO USE

Wear amethyst as a ring or pendant to help you reconnect with your spiritual side. You can also tuck a small, tumbled stone into your pillowcase to promote sweet dreams, or place a crystal on your bedside table to help with dream recall and interpretation.

# Amethyst (Brandberg)

APPEARANCE/COLOR: Transparent to translucent violet with smoky brown
CURRENT AVAILABILITY: Limited availability
PHYSIOLOGICAL CORRESPONDENCE: Ears, nose, throat, sinuses
PSYCHOLOGICAL CORRESPONDENCE: Mental expansion, awareness
KEYWORDS: Spirit quartz, purple fluorite, lepidolite
KEYWORDS: Ascension, personal growth, Ascended Masters, purification

## The Crystal

Brandberg amethyst is a purple, macrocrystalline variety of quartz found only in the Brandberg area of Namibia. These crystals may be found as large single points or as clusters or elestial crystals. Colors range from pale lilac, to bright violet, to deep purple, often with smoky brown areas. The most sought-after Brandberg crystals display enhydros (small air bubbles filled with water).

## Legendary Uses

Although Brandberg amethyst is a recent ineralogical find and has no known specific historical uses, its proximity to the sacred Brandberg Mountain is thought to imbue it with the sacred energy of the mountain's thousands of cave paintings and carvings.

## Attributes and Powers

This is the highest energy of all of the amethyst crystals. Its strong spiritual vibration calls on the Ascended Masters to assist you with big life changes or obstacles. It also radiates with the purifying energy of St. Germain's Violet Flame. Brandberg amethyst helps you to connect to your ancestral roots. It is a stone of consciousness expansion and encourages personal growth and a dissolution of the ego mind. It encourages you to be present in the current moment and let go of attachments from the past or anxiety about the future.

### HOW TO USE

Place your Brandberg amethyst crystal in a place of prominence in your home. It is best used on an altar where you can meditate and connect with the Ascended Masters for guidance on your life's journey. You may also hold it in your sending (dominant) hand and pass it through your aura, like a comb, sweeping away any negativity and dissolving psychic debris from your field.

# Amethyst (Chevron)

**APPEARANCE/COLOR:** Translucent to opaque; deep purple banded with white
**CURRENT AVAILABILITY:** Common
**PHYSIOLOGICAL CORRESPONDENCE:** Eyes
**PSYCHOLOGICAL CORRESPONDENCE:** Open-mindedness, acceptance
**KEYWORDS:** Sugilite, charoite, stichitite
**KEYWORDS:** Spiritual growth, lucid dreaming

## The Crystal

Chevron amethyst is a purple and white, banded variety of massive quartz. The purple bands are amethyst while the white bands are milky quartz. The highest quality pieces are from South Africa, but significant deposits are also found in India. Chevron amethyst is also sometimes referred to as banded amethyst or as Cape amethyst.

## Legendary Uses

This specific variety of amethyst has no known legendary or historical use.

## Attributes and Powers

Chevron amethyst is a stone of spiritual growth and ascension. The pointed, white bands seem to reach upward toward the heavens, a mirror for the human journey toward the spirit. This is a crystal that rules the eyes, both physically and energetically.

It facilitates the opening of the third eye for intuitive development and the acknowledgement of psychic skills. You can use this stone to facilitate lucid dreaming, a state of conscious dreaming in which you can direct the course of the dream. By taking control of the events in your dreams, you may be able to release unresolved issues or negative psychic debris from your subconscious mind.

### HOW TO USE

To use chevron amethyst for lucid dreaming, take a few minutes before bed to hold your crystal while focusing on the issue you'd like to resolve through dream-healing work. If you do not have a specific issue that needs resolving, or if you'd just prefer to explore the dream state, then you can intend to become aware that you're dreaming from within the dream state so that you're able to explore as you wish. Speak your intention aloud or to yourself and tuck the stone into your pillowcase. Picture the stone in your mind's eye as you drift off to sleep with the intention to see the stone from within your dream state, as a visual cue that you're dreaming so that you can take conscious control of your dream.

# Ametrine

APPEARANCE/COLOR: Transparent purple and gold
CURRENT AVAILABILITY: May be somewhat difficult to obtain
PHYSIOLOGICAL CORRESPONDENCE: Brain
PSYCHOLOGICAL CORRESPONDENCE: Grief
KEYWORDS: Amethyst, citrine, charoite, rainbow fluorite
KEYWORDS: Honesty, justice, loyalty

## The Crystal

Ametrine is a natural combination of citrine and amethyst. It is a member of the hexagonal crystal system, but may be found as elestial crystals or in its massive form. The highest quality stones are found in Bolivia, giving the stone its alternate name of Bolivianite. The stone is also known as trystine.

## Legendary Uses

There is a legend that gives the story of Anahi, an Ayoreo princess, who fell in love with a Spanish conquistador. The two were married, and when it came time for him to return to Spain, Anahi was torn about whether to go or to stay with her tribe. There was a fight between the Ayoreo tribesmen and the Spaniards that resulted in Anahi's death. During her last moments, Anahi gave her husband an ametrine stone, the two colors representing her two loves (her husband and her tribe).

## Attributes and Powers

Ametrine's combination of violet and gold colors activate the crown chakra, the body's spiritual center. This crystal promotes honesty and loyalty in all relationships. Ametrine is a stone of truth, including the ability to help you discover inner and spiritual truths. It is an energetic gateway to the world of the spirit and is an excellent stone for psychics and mediums, for assistance in communicating with those who have crossed over. This is especially useful when unresolved feelings or grief is keeping you attached to the person who has passed away.

### HOW TO USE

Write down the name of a specific person or guide that you would like to connect with on a small piece of paper and place the stone atop the paper. Hold your hands over the stone and feel the connection take place between yourself and the spirit, then communicate what you need to say, or listen to messages being shared with you.

# Angelite

APPEARANCE/COLOR: Opaque, gray-blue
CURRENT AVAILABILITY: Available from most New Age stores and crystal stores
PHYSIOLOGICAL CORRESPONDENCE: Eyes, skeletal system
PSYCHOLOGICAL CORRESPONDENCE: Peace, tranquility, serenity
KEYWORDS: Celestite, blue quartz, blue chalcedony, blue calcite
KEYWORDS: Angelic connection, heart connection, oneness

## The Crystal

Angelite is an opaque, blue-gray variety of blue anhydrite. It is a member of the orthorhombic crystal system.

## Legendary Uses

This special variety of Anhydrite was discovered in Peru in 1987 around the time of the Harmonic Convergence. Due to its recent discovery, it has no associated historical uses.

## Attributes and Powers

Angelite is a sweet, soft stone that promotes inner peace, tranquility, and serenity. It helps you to facilitate a connection with beings in the angelic realm. Angelite has a special correlation to the Archangel Michael. This crystal helps to clear unwanted energy from your life so that there are no obstacles to making genuine heart-centered connections to others. These loving connections to those around you create feelings of bliss within you, and they allow you to experience true oneness.

### HOW TO USE

Hold this crystal in your hands or place it on your crystal altar and ask for healing, guidance, and support from your angels and guides. Close your eyes and try to visualize one special angel or guide standing before you, sending pink light into your heart chakra. Feel this pink light balance your emotions and open your heart. Feel your heart connect to all other positive, open hearts on the earth. Allow yourself to open to this energy and feel vast amounts of love and healing pouring into your heart. Send these same positive, love, and healing energies back out to all of the other hearts to which you're connected. Then, share this pink light with your angel or guide and with your crystal to show your gratitude. When you feel ready, slowly open your eyes.

# Anhydrite (Blue)

APPEARANCE/COLOR: Translucent to opaque
CURRENT AVAILABILITY: Limited availability
PHYSIOLOGICAL CORRESPONDENCE: Neck, throat, shoulders
PSYCHOLOGICAL CORRESPONDENCE: Trust, empathy, faith
KEYWORDS: Blue quartz, blue chalcedony, blue calcite
KEYWORDS: Angels, beauty, appreciation, gratitude

## The Crystal

Blue anhydrite is an evaporite mineral in the orthorhombic crystal system. This pale, gray-blue stone forms fanlike blades or clusters that resemble angels' wings. For this reason this stone is sometimes called angel wing anhydrite. The most beautiful crystals of this type come from Mexico.

## Legendary Uses

This stone has no known associated legend or lore.

## Attributes and Powers

Blue anhydrite is a stone of angelic connection. It promotes gratitude and helps you to appreciate what you have, rather than focusing on what you feel is lacking in your life. With this newfound sense of gratitude, you can learn to manifest that which the universe wants you to receive. It promotes feelings of self-worth and deservingness in those who struggle with receiving. Blue anhydrite helps you trust in the universe/god/goddess/spirit and have faith in yourself and your connection to universal source energy. This mineral also promotes feelings of compassion and empathy, encouraging generosity and a willingness to help others in need.

### HOW TO USE

Lie down and make yourself comfortable, place two pieces of blue anhydrite, one over each shoulder, as if they were angel's wings. Close your eyes and feel yourself become lighter, releasing any worry or anxiety that may be weighing you down. Focus on the area of your solar plexus chakra and feel yourself filled with self-love and self-worth. Alternatively, you can place a single stone directly over your solar plexus chakra, aligned so that it is parallel with your spine. Visualize golden light being drawn from the universe into the stone where it pools at the area of your solar plexus.

# Apophyllite

**APPEARANCE/COLOR:** Transparent clear to translucent white
**CURRENT AVAILABILITY:** Widely available
**PHYSIOLOGICAL CORRESPONDENCE:** Endocrine system, brain
**PSYCHOLOGICAL CORRESPONDENCE:** Mental clarity, focus, compassion
**KEYWORDS:** Clear quartz, clear topaz, clear diamond
**KEYWORDS:** Reiki energy, spiritual healing, distance healing, awareness

## The Crystal

Apophyllite is a transparent to translucent mineral that typically forms exquisite clusters or large, pyramid-shaped crystal points. Apophyllite also occasionally forms very tiny crystals, creating sparkling druzes. Apophyllite is part of the zeolite group of minerals and is found all over the world, but some of the best quality pieces come from India. The clusters and druzes are often seen paired with other minerals within the zeolite group. It displays a tetragonal crystal structure.

## Legendary Uses

Because of its unique pearly sheen, or luster, and glassy, reflective surfaces, apophyllite is also sometimes referred to as fish eye stone. This crystal is known as the "reiki master's stone" and is considered a must-have for any lightworker.

## Attributes and Powers

Apophyllite is a powerful stone for spiritual growth and healing. It clearly focuses and directs energy, making it a perfect choice to help you send distance healing. Apophyllite helps to raise your spiritual vibration and move you into higher levels of conscious awareness, especially when used in meditation. This crystal has a strong connection to the soul star chakra found above the head; the soul star chakra is a gateway or connection point to divine energy and universal source.

### HOW TO USE

Hold the stone in your hands for a high-frequency crystal meditation. You may also try placing a piece of apophyllite on your altar or in your sacred space to send healing energy to those at a distance. Alternatively, you can place a natural apophyllite pyramid in the center of a crystal grid for an extra burst of energy and amplification of your intention.

# Atlantisite

APPEARANCE/COLOR: Opaque; lime green with purple-gray spots
CURRENT AVAILABILITY: Limited availability
PHYSIOLOGICAL CORRESPONDENCE: Teeth, immune system, spleen
PSYCHOLOGICAL CORRESPONDENCE: Wisdom, intellect
KEYWORDS: Serpentine, wavellite, pyromorphite
KEYWORDS: Nature connection, fairies, ancestors

## The Crystal

This rock is a combination of stichitite embedded into serpentine. The rocks form opaque, lime green stones spotted with purple-gray to violet blotches. Atlantisite is found in Tasmania, Australia and is sometimes referred to as tasmanite. Both atlantisite and tasmanite are trade names given to this mineral combination, coming from two different mines, but tasmanite is generally seen as being lower quality than atlantisite. The two minerals stichitite and serpentine have also been found together in Morocco.

## Legendary Uses

This stone is named for the lost civilization of Atlantis, but has no known historical or legendary use. Some healers and lightworkers claim the stone can be used to tap into the knowledge of this ancient culture.

## Attributes and Powers

This stone can be used to access ancient wisdom as well as knowledge and information from the Akashic Records. It stimulates the intellect and the mental faculties. Atlantisite can encourage you to reconnect with nature and Mother Earth, especially if a majority of your time is spent within your home or at work. It also calls in the energy of fairy beings and nature spirits. It is a stone of magic and natural healing.

### HOW TO USE

Atlantisite is an excellent stone used in your yard or garden. Place a stone in your yard near a favorite plant or tree. Alternatively, apartment dwellers may choose to place the stone in a potted houseplant. The best way to use this stone is to add it to a miniature fairy garden to encourage fairies and nature spirits to visit your space.

# Auralite-23

**APPEARANCE/COLOR:** Transparent to translucent; deep purple with additional zones of color
**CURRENT AVAILABILITY:** Rare
**PHYSIOLOGICAL CORRESPONDENCE:** Feet, pelvis, skull, immune system
**PSYCHOLOGICAL CORRESPONDENCE:** Harmony, modesty
**KEYWORDS:** Amethyst, spirit quartz, Brandberg amethyst
**KEYWORDS:** Balance, knowledge, cleansing

## The Crystal

Auralite-23 is a special variety of amethyst from the Cave of Wonders in Ontario, Canada. These crystals are quite variable, all with a deep purple body and areas of color ranging from white, to pink, to bronze, or even deep red. They typically form large single-crystal points, or large clusters. Many confuse auralite-23 with Thunder Bay amethyst, but Thunder Bay amethyst crystals do not form the same large crystals as auralite-23, nor do they contain the same variety of mineral inclusions.

## Attributes and Powers

Auralite-23 crystals show remarkable balancing properties, bringing harmony between yin and yang. They can help show you the duality of the world so that you are able to appreciate the joy in the good times and the lessons in the bad. Auralite-23 encourages you to be in balance with the universe, release ego-based resistance to change, and be in the flow of universal energy rather than fighting against it. It helps you to prioritize things in your life so that your responsibilities seem more manageable.

## Legendary Uses

Auralite-23 was named because of the number of volcanic events that helped form the banded layers in these special amethysts. Because auralite-23 has only recently been discovered, it has no recorded historical use.

### HOW TO USE

Hold an auralite-23 crystal in your hands and visualize it glowing with bright, fiery, violet light. See this light expand into your space, dissolving any negative energy from within your aura or your environment. Feel your body return to a state of balance and wholeness, easing into the flow of the universe.

# Azurite

**APPEARANCE/COLOR:** Opaque to translucent; deep indigo blue
**CURRENT AVAILABILITY:** Somewhat common, but crystals may be difficult to obtain
**PHYSIOLOGICAL CORRESPONDENCE:** Eyes, knees, veins
**PSYCHOLOGICAL CORRESPONDENCE:** Acceptance, truth, growth
**KEYWORDS:** Lapis lazuli, afghanite, lazurite
**KEYWORDS:** Intuition, cosmic connections, divine insight

## The Crystal

Azurite is a member of the monoclinic crystal system. It is deep indigo blue and can be found in a range of formations including opaque, spherical nodules and gemmy tabular crystal clusters. The highest-quality crystals are from Morocco, Greece, and Namibia, but the stones are also found in Arizona, France, and Australia.

## Legendary Uses

Azurite was used by the priests of ancient Egypt by painting the Eye of Horus symbol on their foreheads with a pigment made from the crushed stone. It was thought that this would help them to raise their spiritual vibration. Ancient Chinese peoples referred to azurite as the "stone of heaven" and believed that it connected them to the cosmos through a heavenly gateway. The "Sleeping Prophet," Edgar Cayce, referred to this stone as lapis linguis in several of his readings and recommended it to promote intuitive development.

## Attributes and Powers

Azurite is one of the best crystals for honing your psychic skills. It is a natural third eye opener and helps you to both recognize and accept your natural intuitive gifts. If you've been closed off to your psychic abilities, azurite can help you release fear or blocks to activating these innate skills. It can also help you discover your spirit guides and totem animals. Use this stone to deepen meditative states and help you find stillness in the present moment.

### HOW TO USE

Place this stone on your third eye during meditation or place it on your altar or in your sacred space when you're trying to get in touch with your guides.

# Barite (Blue)

**APPEARANCE/COLOR:** Transparent; pale gray-blue to baby blue

**CURRENT AVAILABILITY:** Rare

**PHYSIOLOGICAL CORRESPONDENCE:** Cartilage, thyroid, fingernails, and toenails

**PSYCHOLOGICAL CORRESPONDENCE:** Self-care, patience

**KEYWORDS:** Celestite, blue topaz, aquamarine

**KEYWORDS:** Communication, decision-making, soul path

## The Crystal

This exquisite stone was previously only found in Colorado, until a just few years ago when a pocket of flowerlike clusters of blue barite was found in Morocco. Blue barite is part of the orthorhombic crystal system.

## Legendary Uses

Because of its recent discovery, this crystal has no known historical or legendary use.

## Attributes and Powers

Blue barite helps you to speak from the heart and express your needs. It allows you to communicate to those within your support network when you need their help, even if this is something that you're not accustomed to doing. Blue barite reminds you that you don't have to be a martyr or take the weight of the world onto your own shoulders. Use this stone to show you alternative solutions to difficult choices or situations. Blue barite aids in decision-making and guides you to make the choice that is ultimately best for you. This stone also nudges you toward your soul's purpose so that you can fully bloom into the person you're meant to be.

### HOW TO USE

When you have a difficult choice to make, hold this crystal in your hands and think of all of the potential outcomes of making your decision. Ask the crystal to show you any additional options that you may not be aware of. Sit in quiet meditation with the stone, allowing any possible scenarios to enter your mind. Take time to tune into the stone's energy and request that it help you make the decision that is for your highest good. After your meditation, thank the crystal for its assistance and cleanse it thoroughly.

# Cavansite

APPEARANCE/COLOR: Opaque to translucent, cerulean to cyan blue
CURRENT AVAILABILITY: Limited availability
PHYSIOLOGICAL CORRESPONDENCE: Pineal gland, thyroid gland, metabolism
PSYCHOLOGICAL CORRESPONDENCE: Mental clarity, safety, mental expansion
KEYWORDS: Blue apatite, chrysocolla, shattuckite
KEYWORDS: Spiritual exploration, meditation, spirit guide connection

## The Crystal

Cavansite is an opaque, orthorhombic crystal featuring brilliant blue clusters of needlelike crystals, forming spikey balls. Typically several clusters will be found together on a matrix, either spaced apart in what look like small dots, or clumped together in a mass. Found only in a few places on earth, some of the most striking pieces come from India, usually alongside minerals of the zeolite group.

## Legendary Uses

This mineral was only officially recognized in 1967, so it has no associated legendary uses or lore.

## Attributes and Powers

Cavansite is a stone of spiritual awakening. It encourages you to reconnect with your higher self after periods of spiritual unrest. Cavansite promotes consciousness expansion, especially through meditation and spiritual exploration. This is an excellent companion for journey work and astral travel. Additionally, cavansite can be used to connect with your spirit guides, guardian angels, totem animals, and the Ascended Masters.

### HOW TO USE

Place cavansite on your bedside table. Before going to sleep, set an intention for your dream state. Your intention may be spiritual exploration, astral travel, dream healing, or even connection with your guides. As you drift off to sleep, hold this intention clearly in your mind and feel yourself surrounded by the energy of the cavansite stone. When you awake, record your experiences in your dream journal or crystal journal, if you have one, and try to interpret any messages that you received. If the meaning does not come to you right away, hold your cavansite stone in your hands and ask for clarity in regard to the interpretation. This can be a powerful way to receive messages and wisdom from your guides about important life decisions and your spiritual growth.

# Celestite

APPEARANCE/COLOR: Transparent light blue to gray-blue

CURRENT AVAILABILITY: Common

PHYSIOLOGICAL CORRESPONDENCE: Lungs, back, spine

PSYCHOLOGICAL CORRESPONDENCE: Astonishment, glee, sympathy

KEYWORDS: Blue calcite, angelite, blue anhydrite

KEYWORDS: Hope, faith, warmth, mercy

## The Crystal

Celestite, also known as celestine, is an orthorhombic crystal that typically forms pale blue clusters of glassy crystals on a soft matrix. The most beautiful clusters are from Madagascar, but some collectors also seek out the tabular crystals from Ohio.

## Legendary Uses

Celestite derives its name from the Greek word **cœlestis,** meaning "celestial" in reference to its sky-blue hue. This crystal has no recorded historical or legendary use.

## Attributes and Powers

Celestite is a stone of the heavens. It connects you with the universe, promoting feelings of oneness and helping you realize that you are a part of something greater than yourself. This is a stone of the angels; it helps to restore your faith and encourages you to feel mercy and compassion for all beings. Celestite can promote feelings of elation rooted in spiritual bliss. It is also useful for instilling feelings of hope when situations seem darkest. Celestite helps you to see and appreciate all that you have to feel hopeful about. This is a crystal of warmth and friendship. Use it to help you develop deeper, more meaningful friendships with those who are most important to you, or to help you end friendships that are one-sided or unsupportive.

### HOW TO USE

Celestite is best used in meditation, but it will also work well just by being placed in your sacred space or on your altar. Alternatively, you may take your celestite outside at night (in a safe place), on the evening of a full or new moon. Hold your celestite crystal up to the moon to charge it with energy. Full moonlight aids manifesting and promotes abundance while new moonlight may help you to break bad habits or start new projects.

# Charoite

APPEARANCE/COLOR: Opaque; lavender to purple with some black or yellow blotches

CURRENT AVAILABILITY: Limited availability

PHYSIOLOGICAL CORRESPONDENCE: Bones, bladder, kidneys

PSYCHOLOGICAL CORRESPONDENCE: Determination, pleasure, relief

KEYWORDS: Amethyst, purpurite, stichitite, sugilite

KEYWORDS: Soul-searching, ambition, past lives, enchantment

## The Crystal

Charoite is a member of the monoclinic crystal system. It displays swirling purple and lavender landscapes with occasional black blotches of aegerine. This mineral is found only in the Siberian region of Russia near the Charos River.

## Legendary Uses

This mineral was discovered in the 1970s, so it has no known historical or legendary uses.

## Attributes and Powers

Charoite is an excellent stone to use for past-life healing. It assists with past-life recall and also helps you to release karmic debris or emotional trauma that may have been carried over to this lifetime. By releasing this debris, you can remove fear or negative patterning that is holding you back from discovering your soul path and fulfilling your purpose. Charoite instills determination and pushes you to pursue your goals even if you want to give up prematurely (or if you have a history of not following through on what you start). It's a great companion for ambitious procrastinators. If you feel a calling to pursue a particular career or hobby, but you don't know where to begin, reach for a charoite stone. It helps create the clarity necessary to start new projects or move forward toward your goals.

### HOW TO USE

Place this stone on your third eye chakra and think about patterns or trauma that you'd like to release. Attempt to recall any past lives where this energy may have been imprinted upon your spiritual body. You do not have to relive the negative experience, but rather just simply discover the lifetime where it occurred in order to reassure yourself that it has no practical bearing on your current lifetime. Take a deep breath in, and forcefully exhale while intending to release the energy out of your third eye chakra. Thoroughly cleanse your crystal.

# Covellite

**APPEARANCE/COLOR:** Opaque; metallic indigo to deep purple
**CURRENT AVAILABILITY:** Rare
**PHYSIOLOGICAL CORRESPONDENCE:** Gallbladder, white blood cells
**PSYCHOLOGICAL CORRESPONDENCE:** Sincerity, intuition
**KEYWORDS:** Blue sapphire, royal blue kyanite, azurite
**KEYWORDS:** Divination, enlightenment, restful, scrying

## The Crystal

Covellite is a metallic mineral of the hexagonal crystal system. It's opaque with a deep indigo reflective surface. It is fairly rare with the best pieces originating in Colorado and Montana.

## Legendary Uses

Covellite was named for its discoverer, Nicolas Covelli, in 1832. It has no known legendary or historical uses.

## Attributes and Powers

Covellite engages the intuition and stimulates the activation of the third eye chakra. Its reflective surface can be used as a type of mirror and so is excellent for scrying (a form of divination where you gaze into an object to see images or symbols). Covellite helps you acknowledge all aspects of yourself, even those that are less than flattering, so that you're better able to discern your strengths and weaknesses. This can assist you in recognizing those things about yourself that require growth or change. Covellite can also help remind you to find balance between your home and work life. It encourages you to rest when needed so that you're fully recharged and rejuvenated.

### HOW TO USE

Make yourself comfortable in a place where you won't be disturbed. Dim the lights so that you can soften your gaze and relax your eyes. You may want to light a candle or have a small light source nearby. Hold your covellite stone in your hands and think about an area of your life for which you require some guidance. Begin to look at the stone's surface. Notice its sheen and shimmer. Allow your eyes to go in and out of focus and stare at your crystal. Attempt to see any images or symbols in the play of light on the stone's surface. Once you do, try to interpret the meanings of these symbols as they relates to your question.

# Danburite

APPEARANCE/COLOR: Transparent to translucent; clear, sometimes with cloudy base
CURRENT AVAILABILITY: Available from most specialty crystal stores
PHYSIOLOGICAL CORRESPONDENCE: Neurological system, heart
PSYCHOLOGICAL CORRESPONDENCE: Happiness, peace, hope
KEYWORDS: Clear apophyllite, clear quartz, petalite
KEYWORDS: Angels, creativity, laughter

## The Crystal

Danburite is a transparent to translucent mineral that typically forms large, striated, crystal points. It is sometimes also found in small clusters. It's a silicate mineral that displays an orthorhombic crystal structure. Danburite was originally discovered in Danbury, Connecticut, but the highest quality pieces are found in Mexico.

## Legendary Uses

Because danburite is relatively new to the crystal market, only being discovered in the late nineteenth century, it does not have any known historical uses or associated lore.

## Attributes and Powers

Danburite is a playful crystal that makes you feel light of heart. It encourages laughter and joy and can help to shift even the darkest moods toward happy thoughts. If you're dealing with difficult or negative people, danburite will encourage clear, positive communication without nagging, passive aggression, or sarcasm. It promotes healthy boundaries in all relationships, keeping you safe and protected and shielding your energy field from outside influence. Danburite connects to the sun and moon and is strongly linked to feminine energy and empowerment.

### HOW TO USE

Take your danburite crystal outside on a sunny day. Find a grassy area, a beach, or someplace earthy and take off your shoes so that your bare feet can connect with the earth's energy. Hold your crystal up to the sun and see it filled with light. Feel the crystal store up this vibrant energy and pull your danburite close to your heart. Hold it there, feeling yourself become fully present in this moment, feeling happiness and peace.

# Euclase

**APPEARANCE/COLOR:** Transparent clear, blue, or blue-green
**CURRENT AVAILABILITY:** Rare
**PHYSIOLOGICAL CORRESPONDENCE:** Pineal gland
**PSYCHOLOGICAL CORRESPONDENCE:** Mental clarity
**KEYWORDS:** Aquamarine, blue topaz, blue zircon
**KEYWORDS:** Intuition, psychic gifts, spiritual awakening, spiritual guidance

## The Crystal

Euclase is a transparent, monoclinic crystal ranging from clear, to blue, to blue-green with a glassy surface. These tiny crystals are quite rare. The best euclase crystals come from Brazil, but they are found in many places around the world.

## Legendary Uses

Euclase was discovered in 1792 in Russia. It has no known legendary or historical uses.

## Attributes and Powers

Euclase is a powerful third eye activator. It stimulates the intuition and enhances your natural psychic gifts. Euclase is one of the very best crystals for de-calcifying the pineal gland and ensuring that you are able to remain in touch with your psychic gifts as you age. It is a stone of spiritual awakening and expanded consciousness. It can assist you in getting in touch with your spiritual guides so that you can request guidance on your life path.

### HOW TO USE

Hold a euclase crystal up to your third eye chakra. Take a deep breath in and close your eyes. Visualize pulling blue energy in through the euclase, and into your third eye chakra. Feel the light blue energy of this stone begin to gently dissolve away any mineral deposits from your pineal gland. Take another deep breath in, and as you exhale, release any remaining negativity out of your body. See this negativity being transformed into positive energy as it is sent out into the universe. Intend that only the energy which is for your highest good will remain within your body. Open your eyes and cleanse your stone thoroughly.

# Fluorite (Lavender)

APPEARANCE/COLOR: Transparent; pale lavender with purple edges

CURRENT AVAILABILITY: Widely available

PHYSIOLOGICAL CORRESPONDENCE: Teeth, bones

PSYCHOLOGICAL CORRESPONDENCE: Mental clarity, decisiveness

KEYWORDS: Lepidolite, violet scapolite, amethyst

KEYWORDS: Protection, cleansing, peace, tranquility

## The Crystal

Lavender fluorite is a pale purple variety of fluorite most commonly found in China and Mexico. Fluorite is a member of the isometric crystal system and typically forms clusters of stacked or interlacing cubes. The Chinese lavender fluorite is often tumbled, showing the bands of mauve and pale lavender, while the Mexican lavender fluorite is found in exquisite, rough clusters of near colorless fluorite with deep lavender edges.

## Legendary Uses

Ancient Chinese peoples believed this variety of fluorite protected them from bad spirits.

## Attributes and Powers

This captivating crystal has a light, ethereal energy. It reminds you to take things easy and not get caught up in the day-to-day hustle and bustle. Lavender fluorite is a stone of peace and tranquility. It reminds you to take time to connect with the spirit and can help you create a self-care routine. It's a wonderful stone to have near you during yoga practice or to take to a meditation retreat. If you're studying or learning something new, lavender fluorite can help you focus and concentrate on the information at hand, enhancing your ability to recall even complicated subject matter. It's a great companion for students and teachers alike.

### HOW TO USE

If you're beginning a new spiritual practice, or studying something new, keep lavender fluorite near you. Having the stone in view is a great visual reminder to check in with yourself and be sure you're present. If you start to lose your train of thought or you find your mind beginning to wander, reach out and hold your stone. Take a few deep breaths and remind yourself to focus on the present moment. Feel the crystal's energy help to center you and then return to your task when you're ready.

# Hemimorphite (Blue)

**APPEARANCE/COLOR:** Opaque to translucent, cerulean to robin's egg blue
**CURRENT AVAILABILITY:** Available from most specialty stores
**PHYSIOLOGICAL CORRESPONDENCE:** Coccyx, vocal cords, esophagus
**PSYCHOLOGICAL CORRESPONDENCE:** Joy, inquisitive, thoughtful
**KEYWORDS:** Blue smithsonite, turquoise, cavansite, chrysocolla
**KEYWORDS:** Communication, creative expression, self-awareness

## The Crystal

Blue hemimorphite is an orthorhombic mineral, typically found as a botryoidal mineral crust atop a matrix. The deep, robin's egg blue material is a somewhat recent find from a remote region of China, while the soft teal crystals are typical of specimens from Arizona. Some pieces of hemimorphite have a matte finish while others are intensely sparkly.

## Legendary Uses

Hemimorphite is named for its root words **hemi**, meaning "half," and **morph**, meaning "formed," referring to the strange shape of its crystals. Blue hemimorphite has no known legendary or historical use.

## Attributes and Powers

Blue hemimorphite is excellent for communication. It encourages you to speak your truth, and say what you need to say with both conviction and compassion. It is useful for helping to promote group harmony and cooperation among group members (whether it be at home, work, or within a recreational group). It connects the energy of the sacral chakra to that of the throat chakra, allowing for full expression of creative ideas. If you've had a creative project brewing for some time but have been unable or unmotivated to take action on it, reach for a piece for hemimorphite to help you get started and follow through.

### HOW TO USE

To enhance group cooperation, place a piece of blue hemimorphite in the center of your meeting space. If you need better harmony at home, try placing this stone in the room your family spends the most time in (likely the living room or kitchen). If cooperation is necessary at work, placing the stone in a conference room or office area may be useful. You can also bring the crystal with you to meetings or get-togethers and keep it discretely tucked away in your pocket or purse.

# Hypersthene

APPEARANCE/COLOR: Opaque; shimmering bands of mauve and black

CURRENT AVAILABILITY: Difficult to find, but becoming increasingly available

PHYSIOLOGICAL CORRESPONDENCE: Retinas, sternum

PSYCHOLOGICAL CORRESPONDENCE: Energized, graceful, centered

KEYWORDS: Auralite-23, purple sapphire, plume agate

KEYWORDS: Dynamic, radiance, self-reflection, organization

## The Crystal

Hypersthene is a beautiful mineral displaying flashes of metallic, bronze-mauve on black. The highest quality pieces are from Canada, and although once relatively rare, are becoming easier to find on the mineral market. Hypersthene is an industry name for ferroan enstatite. It is a member of the orthorhombic crystal system, but is typically found in a massive form.

to center yourself and return to present moment awareness. Hypersthene promotes inner-journey work and aids in self reflection. If you're in need of some major soul searching, hypersthene makes an excellent companion stone. Its dynamic energy helps you to get in touch with your inner gifts and shine your light into the world. Hypersthene can also be used to promote organization in all areas of your life, especially during chaotic times when it's needed most.

## Legendary Uses

Hypersthene has no known legendary or historical uses.

## Attributes and Powers

Hypersthene is incredibly energizing. If you're feeling sluggish or lethargic, it can help you feel recharged and alert. It can also encourage you to find times of stillness throughout your day so that you're able

### HOW TO USE

Hold your hypersthene stone in your hands when you're feeling overwhelmed by your day-to-day responsibilities and tasks. Close your eyes and think about all of the things on your "to-do" list. When you have a good mental list, place your stone near you and write down all of the things you'd like to get accomplished. Highlight the things that are urgent and important and prioritize them into an action plan. Hold your stone for a few minutes to energize yourself and then get started with your list.

# Iolite

**APPEARANCE/COLOR:** Translucent to transparent; deep, cornflower blue

**CURRENT AVAILABILITY:** Fairly common

**PHYSIOLOGICAL CORRESPONDENCE:** Eyes, brain, knees

**PSYCHOLOGICAL CORRESPONDENCE:** Revelation, mental expansion, decision making

**KEYWORDS:** Tanzanite, blue kyanite, blue sapphire

**KEYWORDS:** Intuition, direction, guidance, purpose

## The Crystal

Iolite is a gemmy variety of cordierite, an orthorhombic crystal. It ranges in color from cornflower blue to deep indigo. Some of the highest quality iolites come from Tanzania, but this gem is also found in India and Myanmar. Iolite is sometimes referred to as water sapphire, but it is not a true sapphire.

## Legendary Uses

Iolite's name is derived from the Greek word **ios**, meaning "violet." It is thought that the Vikings used iolite's strong pleochroism (the change of color when viewed along a different axis) to help them navigate on days when the sun was not directly visible. As the light passed through a thin slice of gem mounted at the ship's helm, the sailors could tell if the ship was veering off course by the way the stone's color changed. For this reason, iolite is also known as "Viking's compass."

## Attributes and Powers

Iolite is strongly linked to intuition. It instills an inner knowing to help lead you to the right decision when you encounter a fork in the road. It's a powerful ally for navigating life's challenges and is an excellent source of guidance and direction. Iolite can help you discover your life's purpose if you're unsure of what you should be doing. It reveals that which will serve you best and helps you to expand your ways of thinking about the world in order to open your mind to new possibilities.

### HOW TO USE

If you feel as though you're at a fork in the road, write down the different options available to you, each on a separate piece of paper. Hold an iolite crystal above each piece of paper, one at a time, and determine which seems to make the stone shine brightest. This is likely the best decision for you at this time, but listen to your inner guidance as the iolite may be calling your attention to that option for other reasons.

# Jadeite (Blue)

APPEARANCE/COLOR: Opaque, deep gray-blue

CURRENT AVAILABILITY: Uncommon

PHYSIOLOGICAL CORRESPONDENCE: Sacrum, spleen, colon

PSYCHOLOGICAL CORRESPONDENCE: Flexibility, compromising

KEYWORDS: Tanzanite, iolite, sodalite

KEYWORDS: Freedom, relaxation, blessings

## The Crystal

Blue jadeite can be found in Guatemala and California. It is a dark, gray-blue, opaque stone and is a member of the monoclinic crystal system.

## Legendary Uses

Blue jadeite was revered by the Olmec and Mayan peoples of Guatemala, but was not considered quite as precious as the deep green jadeite, even though the blue color is slightly rarer.

## Attributes and Powers

Blue jadeite is an incredibly spiritual stone. Its high vibration promotes independence and personal freedom. Blue jadeite helps to dissolve fear and anxiety about what others think of you, and encourages you to be confident in yourself and in your decisions.

However, it also helps you to see other points of view and maintain an open mind before rushing into things. Blue jadeite helps create a tranquil space and promotes relaxation.

## HOW TO USE

If you're lucky enough to obtain several pieces of blue jadeite, you can use it to create a tranquil space by placing one stone in each corner of a room. Another great way to use blue jadeite is to charge it with moon energy. Jadite works to carry blessings and amplify them for manifesting. Take your crystal outside (in a safe place) on the night of a full moon, which resonates with manifestation. Hold it in your hands, above your head, and up to the moonlight to be charged with the full moon energy. Ask for the blessings of the universe to aid in your manifesting efforts. Carry your charged stone with you to call these blessings into your life.

# Jadeite (Lavender)

**APPEARANCE/COLOR:** Opaque, dusky lavender
**CURRENT AVAILABILITY:** Uncommon
**PHYSIOLOGICAL CORRESPONDENCE:** Tonsils, lips, tongue
**PSYCHOLOGICAL CORRESPONDENCE:** Resourcefulness, joy
**KEYWORDS:** Kunzite, phosphosiderite, bustamite
**KEYWORDS:** Inner strength, generosity, meditation

## The Crystal

Lavender jadeite can be found in Guatemala and China. It's a light, mauve to lavender, opaque stone and is a member of the monoclinic crystal system.

## Legendary Uses

Lavender jadeite was revered by the Olmec and Mayan peoples of Guatemala, but was not considered quite as precious as the deep green jadeite, even though the lavender color is rarer.

## Attributes and Powers

Lavender jadeite is a lovely companion stone for creative people. It can help you express your inner self in nontraditional ways and encourages resourcefulness. It's a stone of happiness and joy. If you're feeling run down or burnt out, lavender jadeite can give you the inner strength to find balance between your responsibilities and self-care (even if you feel like you don't have time). It encourages giving and sharing of yourself with others, but in a way that leaves you energized and nurtured rather than depleted. It can enhance meditation and help you connect to your spirit guides, angels, totem animals, or the Ascended Masters.

### HOW TO USE

Use lavender jadeite to help you develop a regular meditation routine. It can be difficult to meditate regularly, but lavender jadeite provides gentle encouragement. Make a meditation ritual for yourself that somehow incorporates your crystal. Try setting it in a place where you will see it often and use it as a reminder to make time for mindfulness. Or, commit to a five-minute meditation each day for five days. Hold your lavender jadeite at the start of each meditation to help keep you motivated. At the end of the five days, take two days off, and then start up your five-day schedule again. Take time to connect with your lavender jadeite during your two days off to keep you on the right track with your routine.

# Kyanite (Blue)

APPEARANCE/COLOR: Transparent to translucent, cerulean to dark blue

CURRENT AVAILABILITY: Common

PHYSIOLOGICAL CORRESPONDENCE: Spine, muscles

PSYCHOLOGICAL CORRESPONDENCE: Harmony, bravery

KEYWORDS: Blue sapphire, tanzanite, iolite

KEYWORDS: Clearing cords and attachments, balance, alignment

## The Crystal

Blue kyanite is a member of the triclinic crystal system. It ranges from bright cerulean to dark blue and forms long, bladelike crystals. These crystals may be found in clusters or in fanlike formations. The best quality blue kyanite comes from Brazil and India, but it is found across the globe.

## Legendary Uses

Kyanite gets its name from the Greek word **kyanos,** meaning "blue." It is also sometimes called disthene, meaning "two strengths," referring to its variable hardness.

## Attributes and Powers

Blue kyanite is most well known for its ability to harmonize the chakra centers. It can be used to bring the chakras back into balance if they are out of alignment. This stone of two strengths promotes both physical power and mental resolve. Blue kyanite is also a great cleanser and can be used to dissolve energy attachments from those who have hooked into your energy field. It helps set healthy energetic boundaries to prevent others from latching onto you and depleting your energy (whether conscious or subconscious).

### HOW TO USE

To balance and harmonize your chakra centers, hold a piece of blue kyanite parallel to your spine over your root chakra for approximately one to two minutes. Next, move the stone to your sacral chakra and hold it in place for an additional one to two minutes. Continue in this manner moving up through the chakra centers: solar plexus chakra, heart chakra, throat chakra, third-eye chakra, and crown chakra. Once you are finished, take a deep, cleansing breath and stomp your feet to re-ground yourself. Cleanse your stone thoroughly.

# Labradorite

**APPEARANCE/COLOR:** Opaque to translucent; dark gray to black with rainbow schiller
**CURRENT AVAILABILITY:** Common
**PHYSIOLOGICAL CORRESPONDENCE:** Back, hands, feet, ears
**PSYCHOLOGICAL CORRESPONDENCE:** Happiness, joy, security
**KEYWORDS:** Black moonstone, chalcopyrite, rainbow aura quartz
**KEYWORDS:** Protection, clairvoyance, intuition

## The Crystal

Labradorite is a variety of anorthite. The highest quality pieces are from Madagascar, but there are also significant deposits in Canada and Finland. It is a member of the triclinic crystal system and displays a rainbow schiller (typically with gold, green, and blue with occasional pink or orange) on a dark gray to black background.

## Legendary Uses

Labradorite was officially named in 1770 after the Labrador Peninsula in Canada where it was originally found. There is an Inuit legend that describes how the Northern Lights once disappeared from the sky. The Inuit people sent their bravest warrior to recover the lights. He had been searching for a long time when he finally spotted a bright light within the stones beneath his feet. He struck the stone with his spear, freeing some of the light, which returned to the sky, but some still remained trapped within the stones.

## Attributes and Powers

Labradorite is a powerful stone for psychic protection. It acts to shield your aura from outside energy, reflecting the negativity away from you like a mirror. Additionally, it acts to stimulate your intuition, giving you insight into the intentions of those who have your highest good in mind, and those who don't. It is especially connected to clairvoyance, the gift of psychic sight, and can help you develop this skill to the best of your ability. Labradorite works to repair rips or tears in the energy field, restoring the aura to optimum health. When you tune into the energy of labradorite, you'll likely feel instantly happier and more joyful due to its uplifting energy.

### HOW TO USE

Carry labradorite with you or wear it as jewelry for constant protection from negativity.

# Lapis Lazuli

APPEARANCE/COLOR: Opaque; indigo with gold flecks and occasional white blotches
CURRENT AVAILABILITY: Fairly common
PHYSIOLOGICAL CORRESPONDENCE: Heart
PSYCHOLOGICAL CORRESPONDENCE: Honesty, truth, justice
KEYWORDS: Azurite, sodalite, blue sapphire
KEYWORDS: Protection, worthiness

## The Crystal

Lapis lazuli is an azure blue, opaque rock composed of a variety of blue mineral components ranging from hauyne to afghanite with inclusions of pyrite and white calcite. The best lapis comes from Afghanistan.

## Legendary Uses

Lapis has been mined in Pakistan and Afghanistan since 7,000 BCE. It was one of the stones said to have adorned the breastplate of Aaron, the high priest of ancient Israel mentioned in the Bible. The Sumerian goddess Inanna was said to wear a lapis necklace. Inanna also carried long wands of lapis that she used to measure the length of a person's lifetime. The ancient Egyptians used lapis, which they named **chesbet**, for seals, jewelry, and cosmetics. The Egyptian **Book of the Dead** explains that lapis was a powerful protector from evil spirits, so it was commonly used in talismans for the deceased. Two chapters of the Egyptian **Book of the Dead** were carved on lapis tablets. The stone even adorned the funeral mask of the Pharaoh Tutankhamun. Lapis was used as an aphrodisiac in ancient Rome. There is a legend about an angel who gave King Solomon a lapis ring with the ability to control demons, so he used their labor to construct his great temple. The Babylonian peoples had a myth of a great gemstone tree that had leaves of lapis.

## Attributes and Powers

Lapis can be used for protection, truth, and to learn harness your inner power. It stimulates intuition and can connect you with divine energy.

### HOW TO USE

Wearing lapis jewelry to harness your inner strength dates back thousands of years and is still a beneficial practice today.

# Moldavite

**APPEARANCE/COLOR:** Transparent; emerald green to forest green
**CURRENT AVAILABILITY:** Rare, but available from most specialty stores
**PHYSIOLOGICAL CORRESPONDENCE:** Heart, brain
**PSYCHOLOGICAL CORRESPONDENCE:** Bliss, curiosity
**KEYWORDS:** Emerald, green aventurine, green nephrite jade
**KEYWORDS:** Cosmic consciousness, spiritual seeker, journey, mystery

## The Crystal

Moldavite is a green, glass-like tektite formed from a meteorite that impacted an area near the Vltava River (formerly the Moldau River, for which the stone is named) approximately fifteen million years ago. Because it is a natural glass, it has no internal crystalline structure.

## Legendary Uses

It is theorized that one of the stones set in the legendary sword, Excalibur, was a piece of moldavite. A moldavite gemstone is also said to be set in the legendary Holy Grail. Some believe that moldavite was revered by Neolithic peoples as long ago as 25,000 BCE. Moldavite amulets, arrowheads, and blades were discovered alongside the Venus of Willendorf statues found in Austria. One legend describes moldavite's arrival on earth as being the large green stone from the crown of Lucifer that fell from his brow when he was cast out of heaven. There are some sources that relate moldavite to the legendary Cintamani Stone of Tibet or to the Philosopher's Stone of the West. A moldavite rosary was given to Pope John Paul II by the people of the Czech Republic.

## Attributes and Powers

Moldavite is a magnificent stone for all enhancing spiritual pursuits, from meditation, to prayer, to yoga, to ritual, and more. You may use moldavite to fast track your spiritual growth, but be prepared for a wild ride filled with mystery and intense inner journey work.

### HOW TO USE

Holding moldavite during meditation is the best way to use this crystal for spiritual development.

# Moonstone (Black)

**APPEARANCE/COLOR:** Opaque to translucent; dark gray-black to coffee-colored schiller
**CURRENT AVAILABILITY:** Fairly common
**PHYSIOLOGICAL CORRESPONDENCE:** Lungs, neurological system
**PSYCHOLOGICAL CORRESPONDENCE:** Security, nurturing
**KEYWORDS:** Black onyx, basalt, black star diopside
**KEYWORDS:** Transformation, rebirth, spirituality

## The Crystal

Black moonstone is a member of the monoclinic crystal system and is a variety of feldspar. Black moonstone originates in India and displays a beautiful bronze to brown schiller on the surface of deep brown to gray-black stones.

## Legendary Uses

This variety of moonstone has no known associated legendary uses.

## Attributes and Powers

Black moonstone is connected to goddess energy. It is a stone of feminine empowerment and is linked to the archetypes of the maiden, the mother, and the crone. It is an excellent companion stone for times of rebirth or transformation, especially spiritual rebirths. Black moonstone reveals to you your identity as seen by the divine. It can facilitate a connection between yourself and your spirit guides. It is especially powerful for use during ritual or ceremony related to the moon phases. Black moonstone is related to all forms of growth (physical, mental, and emotional). It keeps you protected during major life transitions so that you can emerge safe, supported, and whole on the other side of your journey. It encourages you to give in to your wild side and experience true freedom, following your passions and nurturing your soul, for the highest good of your being.

### HOW TO USE

To truly bond with the energy of this crystal, use it during every major moon phase for one full lunar cycle (new, waxing crescent, first quarter, waxing gibbous, full, waning gibbous, third quarter, waning crescent, back to new). Set aside 5–10 minutes every evening during each phase of the moon cycle to sit and meditate with your crystal, feeling yourself become connected to the lunar energy.

# Moonstone (Rainbow)

**APPEARANCE/COLOR:** Transparent to translucent; white with flashes of blue schiller
**CURRENT AVAILABILITY:** Common, but the prized flawless stones are rare
**PHYSIOLOGICAL CORRESPONDENCE:** Womb, fertility
**PSYCHOLOGICAL CORRESPONDENCE:** Emotional balance, fascination, focus
**KEYWORDS:** Angel aura quartz, milky quartz
**KEYWORDS:** Life cycles, feminine support, gratitude, patience, abundance

## The Crystal

Rainbow moonstone is part of the feldspar mineral group and is composed of both albite and orthoclase, which form in alternating layers, giving the moonstone its characteristic adularescence (the colorful schiller on the stone's surface). Albite is a triclinic crystal while orthoclase is a monoclinic crystal. The highest quality rainbow moonstone crystals are from India and Sri Lanka.

## Legendary Uses

Rainbow moonstone is an alternate June birthstone. It's the gem related to the thirteenth wedding anniversary, which is significant because there are also thirteen moon cycles in a year. Ancient Romans believed that moonstone was made when the moon's light touched the earth and thought that it carried the energy of the goddess Diana. The Greeks also revered the stone, associating it with the moon goddess Selene, Artemis, and Hecate, among others. It is traditionally associated with Mondays (the "moon day"). In India, it was believed that by placing a moonstone in your mouth on the night of a full moon, you could tell the future. In Hindu mythology it is said that moonstone was created from the eyes of the demon Bali when he was defeated by Lord Vishnu. Moonstones are seen as a symbol of fertility in the Middle East and are sewn into women's undergarments.

## Attributes and Powers

Moonstone is traditionally associated with cycles—of life, of fertility, and of crops. It is a powerful abundance stone and is excellent for manifesting. Rainbow moonstone also helps to balance the emotions.

### HOW TO USE

Place this crystal outside, overnight, to charge it with lunar energy on the night of a full moon. Then write down what you'd like to manifest on a small piece of paper and place the charged crystal atop the paper to call your desire into being.

# Nuummite

**APPEARANCE/COLOR:** Opaque; deep brown with shimmering gold flecks
**CURRENT AVAILABILITY:** Very rare, but available from many specialty stores
**PHYSIOLOGICAL CORRESPONDENCE:** Electrolyte regulation, DMT production
**PSYCHOLOGICAL CORRESPONDENCE:** Out-of-body experiences
**KEYWORDS:** Bronzite, hypersthene, astrophyllite
**KEYWORDS:** Spiritual awakening, lucid dreaming, journey work

## The Crystal

Nuummite is a metamorphic rock made of the minerals anthophyllite and gedrite. Its sole location of origin is Greenland, but similar material has also been found in the United States.

## Legendary Uses

Nuummite was discovered in 1982, so it has no known historical significance. It is named for the town of Nuuk, in Greenland, where it was discovered.

## Attributes and Powers

Nuummite is an excellent stone for meditation. It deepens the meditation, allowing you to fully immerse yourself in an inner journey. It promotes astral travel and other mystical experiences and usually comes into your life if you're in a period of great spiritual awakening. Nuummite is one of the most profoundly consciousness-expanding stones available. It can be used to create altered states of awareness for dissolving the ego consciousness and learning about who you truly are at the core of your being.

### HOW TO USE

Schedule a mini spiritual retreat for yourself for an entire day. Plan your whole day, from what you will eat (and having all of your meals prepared in advance), to how you will spend your time. It's important that you make an effort to disconnect from the outside world on this day and focus on inner work. A large portion of your day should be dedicated to meditating in a dark, quiet room, free from distractions. Create a sacred space for yourself where you can connect with the energy of your nuummite stone. Make yourself comfortable and place the crystal on your third eye chakra, allowing yourself to open fully to the experience of the crystal's energy during your meditation.

# Obsidian (Rainbow Sheen)

**APPEARANCE/COLOR:** Opaque; glassy black with a rainbow schiller
**CURRENT AVAILABILITY:** Uncommon
**PHYSIOLOGICAL CORRESPONDENCE:** Heart, lungs, navel
**PSYCHOLOGICAL CORRESPONDENCE:** Safety, mental clarity
**KEYWORDS:** Gold sheen obsidian, labradorite, rainbow aura quartz
**KEYWORDS:** Psychic skills, ancestors, protection

## The Crystal

Rainbow sheen obsidian is a variety of obsidian that includes nanoparticles of magnetite, which are responsible for its characteristic iridescence. It is also known as iris obsidian. Obsidian is a natural glass and has no internal crystalline structure; it's an amorphous mineral. The best quality rainbow sheen obsidian comes from Mexico, but it has also been found in California.

## Legendary Uses

This specific variety of obsidian has no known historical or legendary uses.

## Attributes and Powers

Rainbow obsidian is known for its ability to stimulate the intuition and help you develop your psychic skills. It contains all of the colors in the spectrum and is excellent for balancing and aligning the chakras. Rainbow sheen obsidian is also an excellent protection stone, dissolving negativity from your energy field and repairing your aura. It is especially useful for psychics or mediums who routinely connect with those on the other side, keeping the user protected from entities or energetic attachments. Rainbow sheen obsidian can be polished into a mirror or scrying surface and used for divination, helping you to receive messages and wisdom from your guides and ancestor spirits.

### HOW TO USE

If you're doing any kind of channeling, psychic work, or mediumship, place a piece of rainbow sheen obsidian in a prominent location within your space. Create an affirmation of safety or protective prayer for yourself to keep you shielded during your work. This may be something as simple as, "I am shielded, protected, and secure," to something very specific about the type of psychic work that you do. Hold your hands over the obsidian stone while speaking your affirmation aloud, activating the crystal and filling your space with protective energy.

# Opal (Boulder)

**APPEARANCE/COLOR:** Opaque to translucent; tan with glittering rainbow swirls

**CURRENT AVAILABILITY:** Limited availability

**PHYSIOLOGICAL CORRESPONDENCE:** Fluid retention, stomach, eyes

**PSYCHOLOGICAL CORRESPONDENCE:** Flexibility, happiness, joy

**KEYWORDS:** Chalcopyrite, welo opal, labradorite

**KEYWORDS:** Chakra balancing, peace, hope

## The Crystal

Boulder opals are a precious variety of opal that forms as glittering rainbow veins between brown ironstone rocks in Queensland, Australia. Opal is an amorphous mineral and has no internal crystalline structure.

## Legendary Uses

Boulder opal is the October birthstone. The Aboriginal peoples of Australia have a legend that their creator came to earth on a rainbow to share a message of peace. Where the Creator's foot stepped down to earth it forced the rainbow to touch the ground, creating boulder opal. It is the national gemstone of Australia.

## Attributes and Powers

Boulder opal is an exquisite stone known for its ability to instill peace and hope in the user. You can use it to calm your mind when you're feeling restless or anxious. It replaces tension with joy and ease. Boulder opal encourages you to find things in your life that make you happy and spend more time doing those things. It helps you to see the bigger picture and rearrange your priorities based on what truly nurtures your soul and spirit, rather than pursuits that are rooted in the ego mind. Because of its brilliant rainbow of colors, boulder opal is an excellent crystal for balancing and aligning the chakras. It promotes flexibility in the physical body as well as flexibility of mind, changing the way that you usually think about things.

### HOW TO USE

Hold a piece of boulder opal in your sending (dominant) hand and pass it over your chakra centers, beginning at your root chakra and moving up the spine toward your crown chakra to realign them and bring you an overall sense of wellness and balance.

# Prasiolite

APPEARANCE/COLOR: Transparent; pale mint green to sage green
CURRENT AVAILABILITY: Fairly uncommon
PHYSIOLOGICAL CORRESPONDENCE: Feet, gallbladder
PSYCHOLOGICAL CORRESPONDENCE: Emotional purging
KEYWORDS: Green apophyllite, prehnite, serpentine, epidote
KEYWORDS: Earth energy, fairies, spiritual grounding

## The Crystal

Prasiolite is a member of the quartz group and may display a hexagonal or trigonal crystal structure. It's rarely found with terminated crystals and is much more common in its massive state. Prasiolite is formed when a certain amethyst, containing special iron ions, is naturally irradiated, turning the purple crystals green. It is sometimes called green amethyst or vermarine. Amethyst may be artificially irradiated to create prasiolite, so be sure to ask whether or not stones are natural before purchasing them. It's found in Brazil, Canada, and Malawi.

## Legendary Uses

This crystal has no known historical uses.

## Attributes and Powers

Prasiolite is a strong cleanser and can be used to purge the emotional body of psychic debris and excess baggage. If you have been holding on to emotions rooted in past experiences that are keeping you from moving forward with your life, then prasiolite may make an excellent companion stone for you. It allows you to "clean house" and clear unwanted feelings from your psyche. Additionally, prasiolite is a spiritual grounding stone. If you're active in high-level spiritual work, but have a difficult time keeping your feet firmly planted on earth and your mind focused on the present moment, then prasiolite can gently assist you in getting back into your body. It is also said to attract playful fairies and nature spirits, assisting you in activities that can help heal the earth.

### HOW TO USE

Place a tumbled prasiolite stone on the floor any time you're feeling ungrounded or "spacey." Gently place the soul of your foot into the stone (just enough to make contact, but without applying pressure or creating any sense of discomfort). Keep your foot in this position for about 30 seconds and then repeat the process with your other foot.

# Bluestone (Preseli)

APPEARANCE/COLOR: Opaque; gray-blue with green flecks and occasional peach blotches

CURRENT AVAILABILITY: Rare

PHYSIOLOGICAL CORRESPONDENCE: Brain, heart, womb

PSYCHOLOGICAL CORRESPONDENCE: Wisdom, intellect

KEYWORDS: Sodalite, seraphinite, fairy stones

KEYWORDS: Expansion, oneness, mysticism, history

## The Crystal

Preseli bluestone is only found in the Preseli Hills of Pembrokeshire in West Wales. Preseli bluestone is an intrusive, volcanic rock. It's a form of dolerite comprised of feldspar and augite.

## Legendary Uses

Preseli bluestones were used to construct the inner rings of the sacred site of Stonehenge. Welsh legends credit these stones with a variety of magical attributes and Preseli bluestone artifacts such as axes have been uncovered in Wales. The Pentre Ifan, also known as Ceridwen's Womb, is also constructed of large Preseli bluestones and is said to be a doorway to the world of fairies. The Welsh **Red Book of Hergest** and the **Black Book of Carmarthen** describe how Merlin used magic to move the stones from their origin to Camelot.

## Attributes and Powers

Preseli bluestone is a stone of the ancients. It carries with it the wisdom of generations and the magic of the ages. It is strongly connected with the archetypes from the Arthurian legends and is a symbol of loyalty, bravery, earth healing, and mysticism. Its energy is both earthy and fiery and it is strongly linked with the dragon totem. Although the energy of Preseli bluestone is strong and may feel forceful, it is also well rooted and secure, so it keeps you grounded during use.

### HOW TO USE

Preseli bluestone is best used in crystal layouts. Placing a stone above the head, at the location of the crown chakra, can activate your inner knowing and connection to the ancients. Alternatively, a stone can be placed over the sacral chakra to promote an inward-looking journey so that you're able to explore the depths of your psyche and your relation to the whole.

# Purpurite

**APPEARANCE/COLOR:** Opaque; pearlescent violet to purple
**CURRENT AVAILABILITY:** Slightly uncommon
**PHYSIOLOGICAL CORRESPONDENCE:** Pineal gland
**PSYCHOLOGICAL CORRESPONDENCE:** Forgiveness, motivation
**KEYWORDS:** Charoite, sugilite, amethyst
**KEYWORDS:** Shape-shifting, change, transformation, magic

## The Crystal

Purpurite is a member of the orthorhombic crystal system. It is found in many places around the world, but some of the highest quality material comes from Namibia and Portugal. It forms violet to purple crusts or platelike layers of velvety, satin-like, or pearlescent material on a brown to dark gray matrix.

## Legendary Uses

Purpurite was officially named in 1905 for its purple color, but it has no known legendary or historical uses.

## Attributes and Powers

Purpurite is a highly transformative stone. It connects with the Violet Flame of the Ascended Master St. Germain and burns away impurities in your life to reveal your true spiritual nature. It is strongly linked with the symbolism of the phoenix totem. Purpurite is symbolic of rebirth and transformation. You can use purpurite as a touchstone during a period of major life growth. Purpurite can also be helpful for enhancing any kind of ritual, ceremony, or magical work.

### HOW TO USE

When you're undergoing big changes in your life, keep a purpurite stone with you in your pocket or purse so that its energy remains in your field, supporting you during the transformation. You may also want to sit quietly, holding your purpurite stone, and visualize a mighty phoenix in your mind's eye. See this phoenix surrounded by violet light emanating from your stone. Then, visualize the phoenix growing smaller and smaller and flying into the interior of your stone, residing there to help you through these life changes, acting as a symbol of your personal growth.

# Silica (Quantum Quattro)

APPEARANCE/COLOR: Translucent to transparent; gray-brown with blue, green, and turquoise

CURRENT AVAILABILITY: Uncommon

PHYSIOLOGICAL CORRESPONDENCE: Thyroid

PSYCHOLOGICAL CORRESPONDENCE: Mental expansion, clarity, compassion

KEYWORDS: Chrysocolla, shattuckite, turquoise

KEYWORDS: Earth healing, goddess energy, nature connection

## The Crystal

Quantum quattro silica is a Namibian rock composed of shattuckite, chrysocolla, dioptase, and malachite in a matrix of smoky quartz.

## Legendary Uses

This crystal has no known legendary or historical uses.

## Attributes and Powers

Quantum quattro silica is a stone of nature. This crystal aids in earth healing and is strongly linked with the earth goddess, Gaia. It can help you feel empathy and compassion for all of the earth's creatures, motivating you to work toward sustainability and ecological responsibility in your life. Quantum quattro silica is excellent for promoting mental clarity and expanding your conscious mind so that you're able to see that which is not immediately visible or realized.

### HOW TO USE

Take a piece of quantum quattro silica out into your favorite place in nature. Also bring along a bell or chime and a piece of fruit. Sit down and place your quantum quattro stone on the ground in front of you. Ring your bell or chime to call on nature spirits in the area and ask them to surround you and support you during this earth healing ceremony. Hover your hands over the stone and visualize it glowing with bright light. See this light expand and move deep down into the earth, all the way to the earth's core. Hold the intention to offer the earth this healing energy. Then, offer the piece of fruit to the earth spirits to show your gratitude for their support during the process.

# Quartz (Ajoite)

**APPEARANCE/COLOR:** Transparent; vibrant blue in a colorless quartz matrix
**CURRENT AVAILABILITY:** Rare
**PHYSIOLOGICAL CORRESPONDENCE:** Thymus
**PSYCHOLOGICAL CORRESPONDENCE:** Compassion, gratitude
**KEYWORDS:** Turquoise, celadonite quartz, papagoite quartz
Keywords: Spiritual awakening, cosmic consciousness, communication with guides

## The Crystal

Ajoite is a triclinic crystal. Ajoite quartz crystals are found only in Messina, South Africa (even though ajoite itself is found in several locations across the globe).

## Legendary Uses

These specific ajoite quartz crystals were discovered in 1991 and have no known historical or legendary uses.

## Attributes and Powers

Ajoite quartz promotes attitudes of gratitude and is excellent used for any kind of law of attraction work or manifesting. It can help you open your heart and instills a sense of generosity and a giving spirit. Ajoite quartz is also wonderful for facilitating a connection to your spirit guides in order to open the lines of communication for wisdom and guidance. This is one of the highest vibrational crystals available and pairs well with moldavite for intensely spiritual work. Additionally, ajoite can be used to deepen meditation and promote mystical experiences. It is an excellent companion for journey work.

### HOW TO USE

Hold an ajoite quartz crystal up to your third eye chakra and close your eyes. Begin your meditation and picture yourself in a beautiful crystal cave. Start exploring the cave, which is filled with tons of glittering ajoite quartz crystals. Move through the various passages in the cave until you discover a cavern where your spirit guides are waiting for you. Greet them and ask for their wisdom and guidance about any life issues that you'd like clarity about. Allow yourself to receive any messages from your guides. These may come as spoken words, images, pictures, symbols, or feelings. When you're ready, thank your guides, open your eyes, and return to your everyday awareness.

# Quartz (Angel Aura)

APPEARANCE/COLOR: Translucent to opaque; metallic iridescence on white background
CURRENT AVAILABILITY: Uncommon, but readily available at most specialty stores
PHYSIOLOGICAL CORRESPONDENCE: Cellular and DNA healing
PSYCHOLOGICAL CORRESPONDENCE: Compassion, concern
KEYWORDS: Rainbow moonstone, milky quartz
Keywords: Spirit guide connection, service

## The Crystal

Angel aura quartz is created by placing quartz crystals into a very hot (approximately 1600°F (870°C) vacuum chamber with vaporized platinum and/or silver for several hours. The precious metals bond to the surface of the quartz crystals, giving them an iridescent coating. Angel aura quartz is also sometimes known as opal aura quartz or pearl aura quartz.

## Legendary Uses

Angel aura quartz has not been available for very long, so it does not have any known associated historical or legendary uses.

## Attributes and Powers

Angel aura quartz can help you connect with angels, archangels, and the Ascended Masters. It acts as an energetic gateway to the angelic realm. This stone is excellent for enhancing communication with your angels and guides, especially when paired with angelite. Angel aura quartz helps the communication to come through loud and clear so that there is no second guessing as to the source of the information and wisdom being shared. This crystal is an excellent companion stone for lightworkers. If you're an energy healer or lightworker, try adding an angel aura quartz crystal to your space to enhance the effects of the healing modalities you offer. If you're a healer or psychic, you can also use angel aura quartz to connect with your client's guides and invite them to assist in the session or reading.

### HOW TO USE

To enhance the effectiveness of a healing session that you're performing for a client, place an angel aura quartz cluster on your altar, in your healing space, or beneath the massage table.

# Quartz (Aqua Aura)

**APPEARANCE/COLOR:** Transparent; bright cerulean blue with iridescent sheen

**CURRENT AVAILABILITY:** Uncommon

**PHYSIOLOGICAL CORRESPONDENCE:** Neck, trachea

**PSYCHOLOGICAL CORRESPONDENCE:** Imagination

**KEYWORDS:** Blue kyanite, blue apatite, blue topaz

**Keywords:** Myth, legend, astrology

## The Crystal

Aqua aura quartz is created by placing quartz crystals into a very hot (approximately 1600°F (870°C) vacuum chamber with vaporized gold for several hours. The precious metal bonds to the surface of the quartz crystals, giving them a cerulean, iridescent coating.

## Legendary Uses

Aqua aura quartz has not been available for very long, so it does not have any known associated historical or legendary uses.

## Attributes and Powers

Aqua aura quartz is a stone of celestial energy. It connects you to the continuous cycle of the sun and moon. This crystal is an excellent companion for you if you're studying astrology as it helps to deepen your understanding of the archetypal energies of the zodiac. Aqua aura quartz also has an affinity with the energy of mythical creatures like mermaids, unicorns, dragons, and more. This crystal encourages you to speak from the heart and say what's on your mind with great compassion.

### HOW TO USE

Aqua aura quartz is probably best used as a personal meditation stone. To deepen your connection with your crystal, try meditating with it at least three times per week for one month. Before each meditation session, be sure to set an intention or goal for yourself and what you'd like to achieve (whether it be stillness of mind, connecting with guides, self-awareness, or something else). Keep a meditation journal during this time and take note of any interesting or seemingly significant experiences that you have with your stone.

# Quartz (Dream)

APPEARANCE/COLOR: Translucent; sage green to sea green

CURRENT AVAILABILITY: Rare

PHYSIOLOGICAL CORRESPONDENCE: Immune system, heart

PSYCHOLOGICAL CORRESPONDENCE: Subconscious mind

KEYWORDS: Prehnite, wavellite, epidote

Keywords: Dreaming, astral travel, heart healing

## The Crystal

Dream quartz is a variety of quartz with inclusions of epidote and actinolite that color the quartz a sage to sea green color. The inclusions in these crystals are evenly distributed so that the quartz is colored uniformly throughout. True dream quartz crystals are very uncommon and are found only in Colombia. These are not the same as other epidote-included quartz crystals (which show small to large epidote needles throughout the body of the quartz itself).

## Legendary Uses

These crystals have no known legendary or historical associations.

## Attributes and Powers

Dream quartz is one of the most powerful crystals for dream healing. It can also be used for facilitating astral travel and spiritual exploration. If you're serious about exploring the dream state, then there's no better crystal companion. Working regularly with a dream quartz crystal can enhance your lucid dreaming abilities. This crystal can also help heal heart trauma, both physical and emotional. It supports you during recovery from emotional wounds and helps you to be gentle and patient with yourself during the process.

### HOW TO USE

Place a dream quartz cluster on your bedside table and look at it before falling asleep. When you close your eyes, try to picture it in your mind's eye. Set an intention for your dream state—lucid dreaming, dream healing, or intuitive dreaming. Try to have the crystal be the very last thing you think about before you fall asleep. When you awake, hold your crystal and reflect on your dreams. Write down a few messages in your dream journal (if you have one) or on a piece of paper, about your intention for the night before and whether or not you were able to achieve your dreaming goals.

# Quartz (Faden)

APPEARANCE/COLOR: Transparent; clear with a milky, white line
CURRENT AVAILABILITY: Fairly common
PHYSIOLOGICAL CORRESPONDENCE: Heart, spine, sinuses, esophagus
PSYCHOLOGICAL CORRESPONDENCE: Adaptability
KEYWORDS: Selenite, petalite, ulexite
Keywords: Connection, observation

## The Crystal

Faden quartz is a special tabular formation of quartz displaying a milky white line within the body of the crystal. This line looks like a piece of string or yarn trapped within the crystal and is responsible for the naming of the quartz; **faden** is the German word for "thread." The threadlike line is composed of gas molecules that were trapped within the crystal during its formation. The best faden quartz crystals are from France and Belgium, but specimens can also be found in Pakistan.

## Legendary Uses

Faden quartz crystals have no known legendary or historical uses.

## Attributes and Powers

Faden quartz helps to facilitate connections between people. It can be used during healing sessions to enable healers to better understand the needs of their clients. It is also an excellent stone for promoting group harmony and cooperation. Faden quartz can be useful for pessimists as it encourages a positive mindset. It can help you to be flexible and adapt to changing situations and circumstances. Faden quartz assists you in taking these changes in your stride and fully analyzing a situation before making rash decisions.

### HOW TO USE

To bring harmony among the members of a group, place a faden quartz in the center of the meeting space. Ask that all group members join hands, close their eyes, and tune into the energy of the stone. Have each member in the group speak aloud a positive intention for the group meeting for the day. Feel the energy of the faden quartz embrace everyone in the space.

# Quartz (Golden Rutilated)

**APPEARANCE/COLOR:** Transparent; clear with golden needles

**CURRENT AVAILABILITY:** Common

**PHYSIOLOGICAL CORRESPONDENCE:** Pineal gland, gallbladder, kidneys, hair

**PSYCHOLOGICAL CORRESPONDENCE:** Self-confidence, self-image

**KEYWORDS:** Golden barite, golden selenite

**Keywords:** Energy, cleansing, beauty, sexuality

## The Crystal

Golden rutilated quartz is a variety of quartz crystal that contains inclusions of golden rutile. The needlelike rutile crystals penetrate the clear crystal. The best quality golden rutilated quartz crystals are from Brazil.

## Legendary Uses

Golden rutilated quartz is also known as maiden hair quartz or as Venus hair quartz because it looks like silken strands of golden hair trapped within the crystal.

## Attributes and Powers

Golden rutilated quartz is a powerful cleanser. It quickly works to break up blockages or stagnant energy from within your aura or chakra system and dissolves it into tiny bits that are then transmuted into positive energy. Similarly, it can be used to break up calcium deposits coating your pineal gland, increasing your intuition. This crystal promotes self-confidence and encourages the recognition of your own beauty (both inner beauty and positive thoughts about your body image). Golden rutilated quartz also corresponds to sensuality and sexuality. It can re-ignite passion in romantic relationships, increasing feelings of love and intimacy between you and your partner.

### HOW TO USE

To enhance your self-confidence and create positive thoughts about your body image, stand in front of the mirror while holding your golden rutilated quartz. Every day for one week, speak aloud one thing that you find beautiful or likeable about yourself while holding your crystal and gazing at your reflection. The following week, you should speak two positive traits while holding your crystal. Continue in this manner, adding one new thing each week until you feel confident, beautiful, loved, and lovable.

# Quartz (Garden)

**APPEARANCE/COLOR:** Transparent; clear with green and brown mosslike inclusions

**CURRENT AVAILABILITY:** Fairly common

**PHYSIOLOGICAL CORRESPONDENCE:** Lungs, brain cells

**PSYCHOLOGICAL CORRESPONDENCE:** Curiosity, consciousness exploration

**KEYWORDS:** Lodolite quartz, celadonite quartz, lithium quartz

Keywords: Journey work, meditation, personal growth

## The Crystal

Garden quartz is a variety of quartz containing inclusions of lodolite, lithium, and chlorite. The mosslike inclusions within the clear crystal can range in color from green, to lavender, to brown, to pink, to creamy yellow. This stone is also sometimes referred to as garden quartz due to its plantlike mineral inclusions.

These special crystals can be used to explore the depths of your consciousness in order to bring to light that which requires personal growth and change. These stones are powerful tools for inner work, but also facilitate the exploration of the universe through lucid dreaming and spiritual journeying.

## Legendary Uses

Garden stones have no known legendary or historical uses.

## Attributes and Powers

The vibrant inner landscape of these crystals is a metaphor for personal exploration. Garden quartz crystals are commonly rounded into a lens-like shapes and used for scrying divination and meditation. These crystals stimulate curiosity and inquisitiveness and nudge you to question your perception of reality.

### HOW TO USE

Find a quiet place to meditate where you won't be disturbed. Hold a garden quartz crystal in your hands and gaze into its depths. Allow your conscious mind to slowly give way to your subconscious (your inner self) as you explore the depths of the crystal's inner landscape. Take note of the beauty of the crystal's interior; appreciate how the minerals flow and swirl together, in natural perfection. Let all thoughts slip away from you and lose yourself for a time in the peace of the crystal. Once you have achieved a sense of mindfulness, close your eyes and tune into your own energy. When you feel ready, you may open your eyes and return to the present moment.

# Quartz (Spirit)

**APPEARANCE/COLOR:** Transparent with an opaque core; lilac to gold
**CURRENT AVAILABILITY:** Fairly common, but may be hard to obtain
**PHYSIOLOGICAL CORRESPONDENCE:** Stomach, skull, ears, fingernails and toenails, skin
**PSYCHOLOGICAL CORRESPONDENCE:** Grief recovery
**KEYWORDS:** Auralite-23, amethyst, lavender fluorite
Keywords: Spirituality, feminism, connection

## The Crystal

Spirit quartz is also known as cactus quartz, pineapple quartz, or porcupine quartz due to its interesting formation. These crystals normally display large points coated with a secondary growth of tiny crystals. They are commonly found in intertwining clusters. These magnificent crystals are from only one location in South Africa. Spirit quartz comes in a range of varieties (including clear quartz and smoky quartz), but is most commonly found in combinations of amethyst and citrine crystals.

## Legendary Uses

Spirit quartz is sometimes called fairy quartz. It is a relatively recent mineral find and has no known historical or legendary uses.

## Attributes and Powers

Spirit quartz crystals activate the crown chakra and assist you in accessing divine knowledge about your soul contracts, the Akashic Records, and your life path. Meditating with these crystals can reveal information pertaining to your past lives and will help you to remove negstive karma carried over to this life time from your past life experiences. These crystals are natural abundance magnets and can be used to manifest health, wealth, and good luck. Spirit quartz is also an excellent crystal companion for emotional healing and can be used to reduce the effects of grieving after loss. Additionally, it is a stone for women, evoking femininity and supporting feminism and women's quality.

### HOW TO USE

A spirit quartz cluster is excellent used in the center of a crystal grid for manifesting. You may place a small written affirmation beneath the stone to enhance its effects.

# Quartz (Tibetan)

APPEARANCE/COLOR: Transparent; clear, often with black flecks

CURRENT AVAILABILITY: Fairly common

PHYSIOLOGICAL CORRESPONDENCE: Teeth, bones, skull

PSYCHOLOGICAL CORRESPONDENCE: Awareness

KEYWORDS: Clear quartz, morion quartz, Herkimer diamond

Keywords: Honesty, virtue, serenity

## The Crystal

Tibetan quartz is a variety of quartz crystal found in the Himalayan Mountains. It typically forms short, double-terminated crystals, but occasionally forms single-terminated points or clusters. The most sought-after Tibetan quartz crystals display enhydros (small air bubbles filled with water). These crystals often contain inclusions of black anthracite (coal). These black Tibetan quartz crystals are also highly prized by collectors.

has a deeply spiritual energy and connects you to the heart of the earth. It promotes compassion and empathy and instills feelings of oneness. This stone resonates with the vibrational frequency of the Himalayas, emitting their wisdom and strength. This form of quartz also acts as a gateway to the collective knowledge of the Tibetan Buddhist spiritual tradition.

## Legendary Uses

This variety of quartz has no known legendary or historical uses.

## Attributes and Powers

Tibetan quartz possesses strong amplification capabilities. This stone can facilitate deep meditative states and the expansion of consciousness. This crystal

### HOW TO USE

To facilitate deep meditation and to access the wisdom and knowledge stored in these crystals, place one on your third eye chakra. Take a deep breath in, close your eyes, and feel the energy of the stone begin to gentle pulse on your forehead. Chant the mantra, "Om," and feel the energy of the crystal expand, entering your third eye. Feel the energy continue to grow until it fills your entire body. Remain in silent meditation with your crystal for as long as you like.

# Sapphire (Blue)

**APPEARANCE/COLOR:** Transparent, translucent, or opaque; deep blue
**CURRENT AVAILABILITY:** Available, but gem quality is very expensive
**PHYSIOLOGICAL CORRESPONDENCE:** Eyes, skin
**PSYCHOLOGICAL CORRESPONDENCE:** Jubilance, bliss, devotion
**KEYWORDS:** Tanzanite, iolite, sodalite
Keywords: Purity, beauty, spirituality

## The Crystal

Blue sapphire is a blue variety of corundum. Blue sapphire forms as double-terminated trigonal crystals or as flat, hexagon-shaped stones. Some of the best blue sapphire crystals come from Sri Lanka, but blue sapphire can also be found in Burma, India, Madagascar, and Nepal. Synthetic sapphire is common for gem-grade stones, so be sure to purchase them from a reputable source. Many natural stones are heat-treated to enhance their color.

## Legendary Uses

Blue sapphire gets its name from the Latin word **sapphirus,** for "blue." It is the September birthstone. The ancient Greeks revered blue sapphire as a symbol of the sun god, Apollo. Blue sapphire is one of the stones said to be part of the breastplate of Aaron, the High Priest of Israel. Some legends even claim that the tablets used to for the Ten Commandments were carved from blue sapphire. The ancient peoples of India used a sapphire gem elixir as an antidote to poisons.

Ancient Persians believed that the reflection of blue light from sapphire stones was responsible for the color of the sky. Some sources also claim Solomon's Seal, a magical ring, was set with a blue sapphire gem.

## Attributes and Powers

Blue sapphire is a symbol of purity. It works to cleanse the body on both a physical and energetic level. The gem is also associated with beauty, enhancing inner beauty and physical appearance alike. Blue sapphire encourages devotion, in relationships, to causes, and in spiritual pursuits. It can help you to reaffirm your connection to the spiritual part of yourself.

### HOW TO USE

Wear a piece of blue sapphire jewelry to help recognize your achievements and celebrate them.

# Scolecite

APPEARANCE/COLOR: Transparent clear to translucent white; rarely pale pink
CURRENT AVAILABILITY: Available
PHYSIOLOGICAL CORRESPONDENCE: Skull, spine, brain, neurological system
PSYCHOLOGICAL CORRESPONDENCE: Mental health, emotional boundaries
KEYWORDS: Selenite, petalite, ulexite
Keywords: Cleansing, transformation, spiritual growth, ascension

## The Crystal

Scolecite is a monoclinic crystal, forming clear to white, fanlike clusters of blade-shaped crystals. Small crystals often appear fibrous. This crystal is found globally, but the finest quality pieces, forming large, clear fans, are from India.

## Legendary Uses

Scolecite was discovered in Germany is 1813 and does not have known historical significance. It is named for the Greek word, **skolec,** meaning "worm," in reference to the crystal's tendency to expand and curl when heated.

## Attributes and Powers

Scolecite is a powerful cleanser, as evidenced by its use in chemical filtration. It purges negativity and outworn patterns on a DNA and soul level, clearing negative karma from your field and also from your ancestral line. It offers you the opportunity for a spiritual crucible; it brings difficult things to the surface to be dealt with, but it promises the reward of extensive spiritual growth and ascension.

### HOW TO USE

Lie down somewhere you will be comfortable and can remain undisturbed for a length of time. Place the scolecite above your head at the area of your crown chakra. Take a deep breath in, close your eyes, and ask the spirit of the stone to reveal to you what needs to be cleansed and transformed in this lifetime in order to move forward on your spiritual journey. Allow yourself to dive deeply into the energy of your crystal, remaining in this position for about an hour. Be mindful of any messages or feelings that come through during the experience. When you feel ready, open your eyes, remove the stone, cleanse it thoroughly, and record your experience in your crystal journal.

# Selenite

APPEARANCE/COLOR: Translucent white
CURRENT AVAILABILITY: Widely available, very common
PHYSIOLOGICAL CORRESPONDENCE: Spine, brain
PSYCHOLOGICAL CORRESPONDENCE: Calm, mellow, easygoing
KEYWORDS: Scolecite, selenite, ulexite
Keywords: Cleansing, spirit guide connection, protection, transparency

## The Crystal

Selenite is a form of gypsum and is a member of the monoclinic crystal system. It does occasionally form clear, transparent crystals, but is most often seen on the mineral market in its translucent to opaque, white, fibrous form. The best quality fibrous stones are from Morocco while the high quality, transparent crystals come from Mexico.

## Legendary Uses

Selenite is named for the Greek goddess Selene, the goddess of the moon. It is thought that this name was originally given only to the transparent stones, but it is now also commonly used to refer to the fibrous stones as well. The fibrous form of selenite is also referred to as satin spar. Large, thin sheets of selenite were once used for window panes and smaller sheets were used as eyeglass lenses. The Cave of Crystals in Naica, Mexico, discovered in the year 2000, is filled with giant selenite crystals, some of them hundreds of feet tall.

## Attributes and Powers

Selenite is a high-energy healing crystal. It's best known for its cleansing and purifying capabilities, but it is also a highly protective crystal. This stone can be useful for connecting you with the moon cycle and is associated with things influenced by lunar energy (i.e. the sacred feminine aspect, intuition, and the emotions). This crystal can also help reveal things that are being hidden from you. If you suspect someone is being dishonest with you, work with selenite to help things become clear and transparent.

### HOW TO USE

Hold a selenite wand in your sending (dominant) hand and pass it through your aura to cleanse negativity from your field. Begin at your head, and sweep the energy down toward your feet, removing any psychic debris from your aura.

# Seraphinite

**APPEARANCE/COLOR:** Opaque; pearlescent light sage green to green with silvery-white swirls

**CURRENT AVAILABILITY:** Limited availability

**PHYSIOLOGICAL CORRESPONDENCE:** Liver, ears

**PSYCHOLOGICAL CORRESPONDENCE:** Euphoria, gratitude, kindness

**KEYWORDS:** Green nephrite jade, rainforest jasper, epidote

Keywords: Angelic connection, virtue

## The Crystal

Seraphinite is a variety of clinochlore from the eastern Siberian region of Russia. It is a member of the monoclinic crystal system and is part of the chlorite group of minerals.

## Legendary Uses

This mineral was discovered quite recently, so it has no known historical or legendary uses.

## Attributes and Powers

Seraphinite has an affinity to beings of the angelic realm. It can help facilitate a connection to these beings through prayer during times of great need. You can use it to call on your guardian angels and guides for assistance. It's a stone of miracles and can aid in manifesting and in granting wishes. Seraphinite promotes feelings of gratitude and makes you thankful for what you have. This stone helps you put things into perspective and focus on what's most important in your life. Seraphinite has a lightness to its energy and can help you remember to be more playful and not take life so seriously. This crystal also acts as a moral compass, reminding you to act with virtue and integrity, even if you're tempted by the bad influences of others. Seraphinite is a powerful emotional support stone, keeping you balanced and emotionally stable during times of turmoil.

### HOW TO USE

Hold a piece of seraphinite in your hands and call on your guardian angels and spirit guides. Make a wish or ask for assistance in manifesting something you desire. Place the stone on your altar or in your sacred space. Make time to sit with your crystal each day, for just two or three minutes, to reaffirm your request, until your wish has been granted.

# Shattuckite

APPEARANCE/COLOR: Translucent to opaque; bright cerulean blue
CURRENT AVAILABILITY: Uncommon
PHYSIOLOGICAL CORRESPONDENCE: Thymus, heart, brow
PSYCHOLOGICAL CORRESPONDENCE: Optimism, hope
KEYWORDS: Ajoite quartz, quantum quattro silica, blue hemimorphite
Keywords: Harmony, spiritual ascension, animal communication

## The Crystal

Shattuckite is a member of the orthorhombic crystal system. Shattuckite forms small, sphere-like, blue nodules of radial crystals, typically on a matrix. The best shattuckite comes from Namibia and Arizona.

## Legendary Uses

This crystal has no known legendary or historical uses.

## Attributes and Powers

Shattuckite is an excellent stone for promoting a connection with animals. It enhances your ability to understand and communicate with your pets or other creatures. Shattuckite instills a sense of empathy so that you can better understand what your animals are going through, or how you can help them if they seem to be struggling physically or emotionally. Further, shattuckite is a stone of hope and optimism, helping you to stay positive when times are tough. It also helps you to lift the spirits of those around you and be a supportive light for others when they're down. Shattuckite encourages the rapid healing of physical tissue and is great to use for recovery from surgery or major injury. Shattuckite is wonderful for creating harmony in your environment and is one of the best stones to have present in your sacred space.

### HOW TO USE

Shattuckite can create a positive shift in energy if placed in the center of a room. Put a shattuckite stone on your altar or in your sacred space to create feelings of harmony and tranquility in the room, so that you can recharge your personal power when you're in the space. When used in this way, your shattuckite stone acts as a point of connection to the universe and promotes spiritual growth and ascension.

# Sugilite

**APPEARANCE/COLOR:** Opaque to translucent; bright violet to deep purple, with red/black flecks
**CURRENT AVAILABILITY:** Very uncommon
**PHYSIOLOGICAL CORRESPONDENCE:** Tongue, small intestine, heart
**PSYCHOLOGICAL CORRESPONDENCE:** Compassion, peace
**KEYWORDS:** Charoite, stichitite, violet flame opal
**Keywords:** Love, empathy, oneness

## The Crystal

Sugilite is a member of the hexagonal crystal system, but fully formed crystals are extremely rare. Most material is from South Africa and forms as massive purple stones with red and black flecks. Low quality sugilite can range from a dusky, gray-violet to purple-black. The most sought-after pieces are a fuchsia to bright violet color.

## Legendary Uses

Sugilite was officially named in 1944, so it has no known legendary or historical uses. It is sometimes referred to as luvulite.

## Attributes and Powers

Sugilite unlocks the doorways of the mind. It can help you journey deep into your subconscious to clear blockages that prevent you from growing spiritually. This stone can be a useful ally if you feel trapped in a negative work environment, especially when competitive coworkers are causing problems. Sugilite promotes group cooperation and harmony. It is a stone of oneness, peace, and compassion. This crystal helps you to feel a connection to all beings in this world and encourages feelings of loving support. It helps you to get your ego mind in check and work to raise others up when they're stuck in negative patterns.

## HOW TO USE

To clear negative energy in your work environment, place a small sugilite stone in each corner of the space. If something more discreet is necessary, you may want to create a sugilite spray to mist the space, subtly introducing the vibrational frequency of the stone. Place a tumbled sugilite crystal in a small, glass bowl filled with distilled water and leave it to soak overnight. Remove the crystal and pour the water into a small spray bottle. Mist your work area with the sugilite water to promote harmony and group cooperation.

# Tanzanite (Blue)

**APPEARANCE/COLOR:** Transparent; cornflower blue

**CURRENT AVAILABILITY:** Rare

**PHYSIOLOGICAL CORRESPONDENCE:** Blood, fluid retention

**PSYCHOLOGICAL CORRESPONDENCE:** Mental clarity, tolerance

**KEYWORDS:** Iolite, blue kyanite, blue sapphire

Keywords: Spirituality, admiration, magic, transformation, abundance

## The Crystal

Tanzanite is a cornflower blue, gemmy variety of zoisite from Tanzania. Most tanzanite crystals are heated to enhance the depth of their color, changing them from golden brown to deep indigo. Naturally blue stones are extremely rare. Tanzanite is a member of the orthorhombic crystal system.

## Legendary Uses

Tanzanite is an alternative birthstone for the month of December, instead of the traditional turquoise. Tanzanite was discovered in 1967. Some claim that it was Masai cattle herders that first noticed the unique blue color of these gems. There was a wildfire in the area where the golden brown zoisite crystals were found, and the cattlemen noticed that the heat from the fire had changed the color of the stones to vibrant blue. The Masai revered these stones as gifts from the gods. The crystals were named and popularized by Henry Platt of the famous jewelers Tiffany & Co. in the late 1960s.

## Attributes and Powers

Tanzanite is a high vibration crystal that promotes self-reflection and the asking of deep spiritual questions. It helps you to see the world around you in a new light and gives you the courage and motivation to explore new things. This crystal encourages action over complacency. When this gem comes into your life, it means that it's time to get up off of your haunches and push forward on your journey. Tanzanite fills you with passion for your divine purpose and encourages you to share the story of your journey. It facilitates communication and connection with others.

### HOW TO USE

Tanzanite is best used as a piece of jewelry worn during times of transformation and soul searching.

# Vesuvianite (Purple)

APPEARANCE/COLOR: Transparent to translucent; bright pink to light violet

CURRENT AVAILABILITY: Uncommon

PHYSIOLOGICAL CORRESPONDENCE: Digestive system

PSYCHOLOGICAL CORRESPONDENCE: Calms tempers and anger

KEYWORDS: Kunzite, amethyst, phosphosiderite

Keywords: Being direct, leadership, level headedness, mercy

## The Crystal

Purple vesuvianite is a violet variety of vesuvianite and is a member of the tetragonal crystal system. This rare purple variety is only found in Quebec, Canada. Vesuvianite is also sometimes known by the name idocrase.

## Legendary Uses

Vesuvianite is named after Mt. Vesuvius, in Italy, where the green variety of this stone was originally found. The purple variety of vesuvianite has no known legendary or historical uses.

## Attributes and Powers

Purple vesuvianite is strongly connected to the Archangel Zadkiel because of its color vibration. This stone assists you in uncovering past-life memories and experiences in order to help you learn from them and apply them to your current lifetime. This crystal can also help you to focus on your happiest memories, allowing them to fill you with positive energy. Purple vesuvianite can help encourage your forgiveness of those who have wronged you in some way.

### HOW TO USE

When you're feeling sad or blue, reach out for your purple vesuvianite crystal. Hold it in your hands and try to recall as many happy memories as you can. These can be small memories or reflections on big life events. Hold your focus on the way you feel when reflecting on these memories and allow that feeling to fill you up energetically. Practice this exercise at least once a week as a routine self-care practice, or do it daily during times when you feel you need the extra energy boost.

# Crystals for Shielding and Protection

Your energy body is in a constant state of flux. In addition to being ever-evolving, it is also highly sensitive to the influence of outside energy. Your energy field is part of what helps give you your sixth sense and understand the world around you. However, if you don't take steps to create healthy energetic boundaries, you can become completely bombarded by this outside energy. This lack of shielding and protection can leave you feeling depleted, lethargic, and completely drained. In this section, you'll learn about crystals that can help prevent this from happening, as well as some simple ways to start using them to shield and protect your energy body.

Some crystals can even help to support you energetically to keep your aura clear from outside influence and emotionally charged energy. This keeps you happier and healthier by ensuring that you stay feeling fresh and rejuvenated because you're not depleted. This is especially important to lightworkers, empaths, and psychics who regularly connect with other beings and energy in the environment.

# Amber

**APPEARANCE/COLOR:** Transparent; golden to yellow-orange
**CURRENT AVAILABILITY:** Widely available, but high-quality pieces can be costly
**PHYSIOLOGICAL CORRESPONDENCE:** Throat, stomach, mouth
**PSYCHOLOGICAL CORRESPONDENCE:** Relieve grief, confidence
**KEYWORDS:** Carnelian, yellow jasper, golden tiger's eye
Keywords: Happiness, beauty, tranquility, warmth

## The Crystal

Amber is a polymerized tree resin. True amber must be at least 100,000 years old. It is an organic material and is not a true crystal, so it has no internal lattice or crystalline structure. The finest quality amber comes from Poland near the Baltic Sea or from Colombia.

## Legendary Uses

Amber has been used by humans since the year 8,000 BCE for amulets, beads, and pendants. The ancient Greeks believed that amber stones were the tears of the daughters of Helios, the sun god, shed for their brother Phaethon as he was knocked out of the sky by Zeus's thunderbolts. A Lithuanian myth says that the pieces of amber found in the Baltic Sea are pieces of the underwater castle of the mermaid Jurate. It is said that Jurate, daughter of Perkunas, the god of thunder, fell in love with a mortal man and brought him to her palace. This angered Perkunas and he destroyed the palace with a lightning bolt, chaining Jurate's lover to the ruins. The tear-shaped pieces were thought to be the tears Jurate shed for her lost love. The ancient Chinese believed that amber held the souls of deceased tigers. A Norse myth describes amber as the tears of Freya, shed for her lost love Odur, god of the sun.

## Attributes and Powers

Amber carries the light of the sun. It is a stone of warmth and abundance, promoting growth (physical, mental, and emotional). Amber is an excellent companion stone if you're grieving or feel ashamed of your actions. It helps you accept the past and maintain a positive outlook on the future.

### HOW TO USE

To overcome grief or shame, wear an amber pendant on a long chain so that it hangs over the solar plexus chakra.

# Astrophyllite

APPEARANCE/COLOR: Opaque; metallic bronze
CURRENT AVAILABILITY: Uncommon
PHYSIOLOGICAL CORRESPONDENCE: Gallbladder, bowels
PSYCHOLOGICAL CORRESPONDENCE: Authenticity, loving kindness
KEYWORDS: Nuummite, covellite
Keywords: Lightworkers, expansion

## The Crystal

Astrophyllite is a member of the triclinic crystal system. It forms sprays of fanlike, metallic, bronze crystals on a matrix. Some of the most beautiful pieces are from Russia.

## Legendary Uses

This stone has no known legendary or historical uses.

## Attributes and Powers

Astrophyllite is a stone for lightworkers. You can use it to expand your consciousness and help you tap into universal source energy and reveal your role in the great cosmic drama. Astrophyllite activates your light body and temporarily raises your energetic vibration, moving you closer to enlightenment. It is a highly energizing crystal and is good for combating lethargy and fatigue. This crystal helps you recognize the wonders of nature all around you, from the tiniest grain of sand to the most magnificent animal.

Astrophyllite promotes loving kindness and deep states of mindfulness. It also encourages you to step into your authentic self, removing any ego-based ideals of who you are.

### HOW TO USE

Make yourself comfortable in a place where you will not be disturbed; your sacred space or a place in nature make excellent locations for this practice. Take your stone in your hands and close your eyes. Visualize yourself becoming grounded and firmly rooted into the earth. See your light body begin to separate from your physical form, gently rising to the space above your head. Journey with your light body while keeping your physical form grounded. Take your light body through the earth's atmosphere, out into space, past the stars, past the galaxies, until you reach the very center of the universe. Feel your ego self dissolve away from your being and get in touch with the true essence of your being. When you feel ready, take this true essence of self back down to earth and feel it merge once again with your physical body, reaffirming your true, authentic self.

# Avalonite

APPEARANCE/COLOR: Translucent to opaque, pale blue with druzy surface
CURRENT AVAILABILITY: Limited availability
PHYSIOLOGICAL CORRESPONDENCE: Eyes, throat, ears, lungs
PSYCHOLOGICAL CORRESPONDENCE: Courage, bravery
KEYWORDS: Blue lace agate, angelite, blue calcite
Keywords: Inner strength, loyalty, honor, equality

## The Crystal

Avalonite is the name given to a druzy variety of pale blue chalcedony. Chalcedony is a type of cryptocrystalline quartz and displays no outward crystal structure. With avalonite, however, tiny druzy crystals coat the surface of the blue chalcedony stone, giving it a glittering appearance. This druzy blue chalcedony avalonite should not be confused with banded peach zoisite, a trademarked stone of the same name.

## Legendary Uses

Although the stone itself does not have any known historical use, it is named after the mythical land of Avalon, the magical island from the legends of King Arthur. Avalon is associated with healing, power, and magnificent abundance.

## Attributes and Powers

Avalonite is a stone that can transform you from one who needs protecting into a protector yourself. It instills a sense of bravery and courage and can remind you of the strength you hold inside of yourself. It is also a symbol of loyalty, honor, and equality, calling upon imagery from the Knights of the Round Table in the Arthurian legends. It promotes honor in your words as well as your actions and holds you to a code of heroic conduct. It also helps you to command respect in situations that require a natural leader to take control.

### HOW TO USE

This stone is best used when worn as jewelry over your heart chakra or when held in your dominant hand, as if it were a shield. It can also be held over the third eye chakra during meditation to call upon the strength and wisdom from the legendary figures of Avalon and Camelot.

# Aventurine (White)

APPEARANCE/COLOR: Opaque; pearlescent silvery white
CURRENT AVAILABILITY: Common, but may be difficult to find for sale
PHYSIOLOGICAL CORRESPONDENCE: Brain, skin, sensory cues
PSYCHOLOGICAL CORRESPONDENCE: Virtue, removes anxiety
KEYWORDS: Milky quartz, white onyx, silver mica
Keywords: Spiritual expansion, meditation, yoga

## The Crystal

White aventurine is a variety of quartz with inclusions of glittering silver mica. This glittering sheen is referred to as aventurescence. This stone is found in a massive formation. The best quality white aventurine comes from India, but it can also be found in China.

## Legendary Uses

This white variety of aventurine has no known legendary or historical uses.

## Attributes and Powers

White aventurine is representative of spiritual detachment. Working with this crystal can help you to accept the impermanence of all things. This stone shows you how to remove regret about the past and anxiety about the future. White aventurine encourages present moment awareness and dissolution of the ego consciousness. This crystal promotes purity of mind and encourages virtuous actions. It can help you get into the routine of a spiritual practice that's meaningful to you; this may be religious ceremony, yoga, meditation, healing work, or whatever resonates with you best. White aventurine also encourages deep self-reflection.

### HOW TO USE

Use several pieces of white aventurine, one in each corner of a room, to create a sacred space for your spiritual practice. After placing the stones, stand in the center of the room and visualize the crystals connected by lines of energy, linking them together so that they act in harmony. Use this space for meditation, yoga, or religious ceremony to deepen your spiritual work and keep you motivated to keep up on your practice.

# Bytownite

APPEARANCE/COLOR: Transparent yellow-gold

CURRENT AVAILABILITY: Rare, not readily available but may be found at specialty stores

PHYSIOLOGICAL CORRESPONDENCE: Lungs, eyes

PSYCHOLOGICAL CORRESPONDENCE: Happiness, joy, relief

KEYWORDS: Libyan desert glass, citrine, lemon topaz

Keywords: Psychic shielding, assertiveness, personal power, soul contracts

## The Crystal

Bytownite, or golden labradorite, is a gemmy variety of feldspar. It is transparent yellow to deep gold in color. Bytownite is found as massive, rough stones, but displays triclinic crystal symmetry on a microscopic level.

## Legendary Uses

Bytownite was not officially described and identified until 1835, so no known legend or lore exists for this stone. The deposit found in the area for which the stone was originally named has since been lost.

## Attributes and Powers

Bytownite is a stone of higher purpose. It is a highly protective crystal, removing psychic debris and other unnecessary energy from your field so that you remain clear and focused. Bytownite supports you, protecting your energy body so that you have the confidence required to stand in your power and be assertive about your needs on a soul level. This stone also helps to remove negative karma carried into this lifetime from past-life soul contracts.

### HOW TO USE

Hold a bytownite stone over your solar plexus chakra and take a deep breath. Feel the energy of the crystal dissolving any psychic debris, negative karma, or unwanted energy from your physical body. Gently exhale. One your next inhalation, feel the stone's energy extend into your aura and chakra centers, removing any ties to soul contracts that will not serve your purpose for this lifetime. Feel all cords and attachments being dissolved. As you exhale, breathe out any remaining negativity. Feel the energy filling your physical and energetic bodies with golden light, creating a shield of protective energy around you. Breathe in again, this time feeling yourself become empowered on a physical, emotional, and spiritual level. Hold this energy in your being for a count of three. Exhale gently. Cleanse the stone thoroughly.

# Calcite (Golden)

APPEARANCE/COLOR: Translucent; soft yellow to deep gold
CURRENT AVAILABILITY: Common
PHYSIOLOGICAL CORRESPONDENCE: Skeletal system, teeth, digestive system
PSYCHOLOGICAL CORRESPONDENCE: Self-confidence, courage
KEYWORDS: Bytownite, Libyan desert glass, citrine
Keywords: Willpower, physical protection, good health

## The Crystal

Golden calcite is typically found as bright yellow, rhombohedral crystals full of rainbows. Calcite is a member of the trigonal crystal system. The best quality golden calcite rhombohedrons are from Mexico, but this crystal may be found in many other formations all around the world.

## Legendary Uses

Golden calcite has no known legendary or historical uses.

## Attributes and Powers

Golden calcite is a stone of self-confidence and courage. If you're being victimized or bullied by someone, this stone can help to give you the inner strength needed to face your fears and stand up to them. Golden calcite's potent energy fills your aura with strong vibrations of strength, helping you to set healthy boundaries with others. It sends out subtle messages that you will not allow yourself to be taken advantage of or mistreated in any way. This makes it a highly protective stone, working to shield you from hurt feelings or emotional distress caused by others. Golden calcite is also beneficial for preventative protection, working as a sort of good luck charm to keep you free from physical harm.

### HOW TO USE

Golden calcite works most effectively as a protective stone if it is carried with you continuously. Keeping the stone in your pocket, or having it specially wire-wrapped into a crystal pendant would be a simple way to keep its energetic vibration in your auric field at all times. To amp up the energy and effects of your stone, you may choose to create a protective prayer, or confidence-boosting affirmation, and speak it aloud each time you use the crystal.

# Cross Stone

**APPEARANCE/COLOR:** Opaque; peachy pink with black cross-like markings
**CURRENT AVAILABILITY:** Fairly common
**PHYSIOLOGICAL CORRESPONDENCE:** Eyes, heart
**PSYCHOLOGICAL CORRESPONDENCE:** True love
**KEYWORDS:** Bustamite, peach feldspar, rhodonite
**Keywords:** Protection from the evil eye

## The Crystal

Cross stone is also known as chiastolite and is a variety of andalusite. This stone is easily recognized by its peachy pink crystals with dark cross-like markings. The cross-shaped formations are caused by inclusions of carbon within the andalusite. The finest quality cross stones come from China and Australia, but these crystals have also been found in Spain and the United States. These crystals should not be confused with staurolite fairy crosses, which are also sometimes referred to as cross stone.

## Legendary Uses

The name chiastolite comes from the Greek word **chiastos,** meaning "cross-marked." There is a legend from the Araucanian peoples of Chile and Argentina that describes that the dark cross-like markings on these stones are the souls of Araucanian warriors killed by Spanish conquistadors. There is another story from this culture attributing the stones to the tears of a Spanish girl who fell in love with an Araucanian tribe member. They were separated by disapproving members of the tribe and she cried many tears of grief

for her lost love, which solidified as cross stones. The tribespeople saw this miracle as proof of the girl's love and allowed the couple to live in peace together. It is also said that Christopher Columbus wore a chiastolite talisman for protection during his voyage to the Americas.

## Attributes and Powers

Cross stone is a highly protective stone, keeping you safe from both physical and energetic threats to your well-being. It provides protection from the malicious acts of others and keeps you unharmed by the negative effects of the "evil eye."

### HOW TO USE

Keep a piece of cross stone in a pocket on the receiving (nondominant) side of your body to fully absorb this stone's protective qualities.

# Diopside (Black Star)

APPEARANCE/COLOR: Opaque; black with a chatoyant, starry asterism
CURRENT AVAILABILITY: Uncommon, but available from most specialty stores
PHYSIOLOGICAL CORRESPONDENCE: Brow, soles of the feet
PSYCHOLOGICAL CORRESPONDENCE: Intuition, security
KEYWORDS: Black onyx, black obsidian, black moonstone
Keywords: Star beings, magnetism, law of attraction, psychic protection

## The Crystal

Diopside is a member of the monoclinic crystal group. Black star diopside typically displays a four-rayed asterism on a black surface, caused by inclusions of magnetite. Some of these gems contain so much magnetite that they display slight magnetism. The finest quality black star diopside crystals come from India, so it is sometimes called the "Black Star of India," but small deposits of the stone have also been found in a few other locations across the globe.

## Legendary Uses

Black star diopside has no known historical or legendary uses.

## Attributes and Powers

Black star diopside helps to keep you grounded and rooted into the earth during psychic or intuitive work. Remaining properly grounded and centered is important to keeping yourself protected from outside forces of energy when connecting with other realms or beings. Black star diopside helps you to create a protective shield of energy around you at all times. Because of this crystal's natural magnetism, it makes the perfect crystal companion for law of attraction work. Black star diopside assists you in manifesting what which you need most in your life. It will not help you to acquire meaningless materialistic things, but will instead draw in the people or things that are for the highest good of your being.

### HOW TO USE

Wearing a black star diopside pendant will help to keep you safe and protected during channeling or other intuitive work. Alternatively, using a black star diopside stone in the center of a crystal grid can really amplify your manifesting efforts.

# Garnet (Spessartine)

APPEARANCE/COLOR: Transparent; vibrant orange to red-orange
CURRENT AVAILABILITY: Limited availability
PHYSIOLOGICAL CORRESPONDENCE: Spleen, sacrum, ribs
PSYCHOLOGICAL CORRESPONDENCE: Motivation, creativity
KEYWORDS: Carnelian, amber, tangerine calcite
Keywords: Physical protection, emotional shielding

## The Crystal

Spessartine garnet is a member of the isometric crystal system. The finest quality crystals come from Brazil, Namibia, Nigeria, and China. The Brazilian spessartines are deep red-orange and display a naturally etched crystal formation. The vibrant orange gems form other locations most frequently form gorgeous dodecahedral shapes. This crystal is sometimes known as mandarin garnet for its intensely orange color.

relating to the internal organs. However, its true protective abilities lie in its tendency to shield you from the intense emotional energy of others. If you're an empath and find that you're easily influenced by other people's moods or energy, then spessartine garnet makes an excellent crystal companion. This crystal prevents you from soaking up other people's negativity like a sponge, and helps you set and keep healthy boundaries in place for your own self-protection.

## Legendary Uses

This specific variety of garnet has no known legendary or historical uses.

## Attributes and Powers

Spessartine garnet is an excellent stone for highly creative people. It allows you to tap into your emotions and use them as a source of inspiration for your work. This crystal also keeps you motivated so that you're excited to follow through on your projects. Spessartine garnet can be used for physical protection, especially

### HOW TO USE

If you're an empath or find that you're just sensitive to the energy of others, try 5–10 minutes each day to hold your spessartine garnet as soon as you wake up. Focus on breathing in the energy of the stone and visualize it filling your aura. This will allow the energy of the stone to create a protective shield around your auric field so that you remain protected throughout your day.

# Halite (Blue)

APPEARANCE/COLOR: Transparent; clear to deep indigo blue

CURRENT AVAILABILITY: Increasingly uncommon

PHYSIOLOGICAL CORRESPONDENCE: Brain, electrolyte regulation, fluid retention

PSYCHOLOGICAL CORRESPONDENCE: Mental clarity

KEYWORDS: Tanzanite, iolite, blue kyanite

Keywords: Cleansing, spiritual protection

## The Crystal

Blue halite is a member of the isometric crystal system and forms transparent, colorless cubes with streaks of deep indigo blue. The prized deep blue specimens come from New Mexico, Germany, and Canada. The blue color in these stones is caused by defects within the crystal lattice.

## Legendary Uses

This crystal has no known legendary or historical uses.

## Attributes and Powers

Blue halite is known for its cleansing and purifying properties. It works to remove psychic debris and stored negative emotional charges from your aura. It is a highly protective stone and is especially useful for keeping you safe during journey work, astral travel, and connection with dream emissaries. Blue halite is also useful for providing mental clarity so that you're better able to stay focused on the present moment. Being centered works preventatively to keep you protected from the negative influence of outside influences. The deep blue color of these crystals also stimulates your psychic skills, triggering automatic psychic protection and shielding of your aura if you encounter someone who tries to leach your energy (whether consciously or subconsciously). Blue halite is excellent for dissolving energetic cords and attachments.

### HOW TO USE

Hold a piece of blue halite in your sending (dominant) hand and pass it through your aura making small, counterclockwise circles. This helps to draw negativity from your field and dissolve any cords or connections that may be infringing upon your energy. Alternatively, you can place the stone in your sacred space to keep it clear of negativity.

# Halite (Pink)

APPEARANCE/COLOR: Transparent to translucent; soft pink

CURRENT AVAILABILITY: Increasingly uncommon

PHYSIOLOGICAL CORRESPONDENCE: Heart, electrolyte regulation, fluid retention

PSYCHOLOGICAL CORRESPONDENCE: Compassion, emotional balance

KEYWORDS: Rose quartz, kunzite, morganite

Keywords: Heart healing, cooperation, love

## The Crystal

Pink halite is a member of the isometric crystal system and forms translucent, pale pink cubes. The best specimens come from California. The pink color in these stones is caused by algal bacteria.

## Legendary Uses

This crystal has no known legendary or historical uses.

## Attributes and Powers

Pink halite is a great stone for romantic relationships. It works to cleanse negative energy and remove emotionally charged energy from your space that may otherwise contribute to arguments. This crystal also heals emotional wounds and works to heal the heart so that you can trust your partner and have an open and honest relationship. Pink halite promotes compassion and tenderness. It also encourages emotional balance and forgiveness. This crystal is excellent for cooperation, so it helps create compromise in relationships for the highest good of all involved. It is a stone representing true love and allows both you and your partner to be yourselves without judgment or fear.

### HOW TO USE

Place a pink halite in your bedroom or somewhere you spend a great deal of time with your partner. If your partner is open to working with crystals try performing the following technique together. Both you and your partner should sit together on your floor or your bed with the crystal placed between you. Hold hands with your partner, your right hand in their left, and your left hand in their right, above the crystal. You should both close your eyes and tune in to one another's energetic frequency. Hold the intention of ultimate compassion and understanding while you work to connect to the other person. Stay in this state for about five minutes. Open your eyes and share a bit about the experience with one another.

# Heliodor

**APPEARANCE/COLOR:** Transparent to translucent; pale yellow to deep gold
**CURRENT AVAILABILITY:** Uncommon
**PHYSIOLOGICAL CORRESPONDENCE:** Stomach, digestive system
**PSYCHOLOGICAL CORRESPONDENCE:** Confidence
**KEYWORDS:** Citrine, yellow topaz, amber
**Keywords:** Power, strength

## The Crystal

Heliodor is a yellow to gold variety of beryl. It displays a hexagonal crystal system and may be transparent to translucent. It is found in many locations across the globe, but some of the best specimens come from Brazil, Pakistan, France, and Namibia. This mineral is often artificially created by irradiating aquamarine crystals, so be sure to purchase from a reputable dealer if you prefer natural stones.

## Legendary Uses

This crystal was first discovered in Namibia in 1910. It is named for the Greek word **helios**, meaning "sun," and the word **doron**, meaning "gift," as it was seen as a gift from the sun. Because of its fairly recent discovery, there are no known legendary or historical uses for this gem.

## Attributes and Powers

Heliodor has a bright, sunny energy and can help you to turn a sour mood into a cheerful one. It quickly works to activate your solar plexus chakra, the powerhouse of the chakra system, to energize you if you're feeling lethargic or tired. It also combats chronic exhaustion or fatigue. Heliodor is highly protective due to its connection to the solar plexus, the center for personal power. It helps you set boundaries and stand in your power, keeping you safe from the negativity or manipulations of others. It is a very masculine energy stone and is a great companion for those in leadership positions, as it helps you to be firm and direct while maintaining compassion and egolessness.

### HOW TO USE

Heliodor is best used by wearing it as a pendant on a long chain so that it hangs over the area of the solar plexus chakra.

# Jasper (Kambaba)

**APPEARANCE/COLOR:** Opaque, sage green with deep green to black swirls or spots
**CURRENT AVAILABILITY:** Common
**PHYSIOLOGICAL CORRESPONDENCE:** Abdomen, feet, pelvis
**PSYCHOLOGICAL CORRESPONDENCE:** Safety, security
**KEYWORDS:** Rainforest jasper, Preseli bluestone, bloodstone
Keywords: Protection, grounding, earth connection and healing

## The Crystal

It is hotly debated whether kambaba jasper (also known as crocodile jasper) is a true jasper, a form of rhyolite, or a type of stromatolite fossil. It is certainly composed of silicate minerals, but the further details of its composition are yet unknown.

## Legendary Uses

There are no known legendary uses of kambaba jasper.

## Attributes and Powers

Kambaba jasper is an intensely grounding and protective stone. The many small spots on its surface look like tiny eyes, keeping watch over you and protecting you from physical and emotional harm. This stone is excellent as a talisman to ward off the evil eye, and will keep those who drain your energy at bay. The energy of this stone allows you to relax into otherwise tense surroundings and is especially supportive in hostile workplaces. Additionally, this stone calls upon fairies and other earth spirits to keep you safe and secure in all aspects of your life.

### HOW TO USE

Take a piece of kambaba jasper out into nature. Find a place where you feel comfortable and happy, perhaps beneath a tree, in a wildflower meadow, or on the beach. Hold the stone in your hands and request that any nearby nature spirits gather around you. Speak your request for protection to these fairies and other beings and ask that they work with the energy of the stone to support you, keeping you safe and secure. It's best to make your request for protection as specific to your situation as possible, but requesting general protection from the universe is also beneficial. Thank the nature spirits for hearing and responding to your request.

# Jasper (Orbicular)

APPEARANCE/COLOR: Translucent to opaque; all colors, but predominantly green and white
CURRENT AVAILABILITY: Increasingly uncommon
PHYSIOLOGICAL CORRESPONDENCE: Fluid retention, heart, lungs, throat
PSYCHOLOGICAL CORRESPONDENCE: Creativity
KEYWORDS: Mexican lace agate, rainforest jasper
Keywords: Mermaids, Mother Earth, water element

## The Crystal

Orbicular jasper (also known as ocean jasper) is a variety of the mineral rhyolite and displays radial, sphere-like inclusions of quartz and feldspar crystals. The main body of these stones typically ranges from green to white, but they may come in any hue, displaying beautiful, ringed dots of color including yellow, pink, blue, or even orange. The characteristic ringed dots is difficult to distinguish on rough stones, so the crystals are typically cut into slabs or polished into spheres to tumbled stones to fully display the magnificent patterns. Orbicular jasper was found in a single location on the coast of Madagascar, and could only be mined during low tide. The Madagascar deposit was found in 1999, but mining ceased in 2006 when the deposit was depleted. Similar material, of lower quality, has been found in a few other locations around the world. This crystal is sometimes known as sea jasper, fish eye jasper, or as the Atlantis stone (not to be confused with atlantisite or with larimar, which is also known as the Atlantis stone).

## Legendary Uses

Orbicular jasper is a relatively recent discovery and has no known legendary or historical uses.

## Attributes and Powers

Orbicular jasper is a stunning stone that connects you with the water element and the energy of the sea. It facilitates communication with mermaid guides and enhances the clarity of intuitive messages received from nature and Mother Earth.

### HOW TO USE

Hold this stone while meditating near any body of water to tune in to the energy of the water element and to strengthen your intuition.

# Kyanite (Black)

**APPEARANCE/COLOR:** Opaque; dark charcoal gray to black
**CURRENT AVAILABILITY:** Common
**PHYSIOLOGICAL CORRESPONDENCE:** Lungs, bladder
**PSYCHOLOGICAL CORRESPONDENCE:** Alleviates fear and anxiety, reduces stress
**KEYWORDS:** Black onyx (shungite), basalt
Keywords: Protection from psychic attack, aura repair, chakra balancing, grounding

## The Crystal

Black kyanite is a member of the triclinic crystal system. It ranges from dark, charcoal gray to black and forms fanlike crystal shapes. Black kyanite is only found in Brazil.

## Legendary Uses

Kyanite is sometimes called disthene, meaning "two strengths," referring to its variable hardness. Black kyanite has no known legendary or historical uses.

## Attributes and Powers

Black kyanite is a highly protective stone. It helps to keep you grounded so that your natural protective shields are active. Further, this crystal can help to keep you safe from psychic attack or from the ill-wishing of others. Black kyanite assists with balancing and aligning your chakra centers and can even be used to repairs tears, holes, or leaks in your aura. It is a great stress reducer and helps you let go of emotional and psychic baggage that are negatively impacting your physical health. If you're feeling anxious or afraid, black kyanite works to get you centered and focused on the present moment so that you can release the anxiety and take control of your emotions.

### HOW TO USE

If you're feeling anxious or stressed, hold black kyanite in your sending (dominant) hand and use it to sweep through your aura. Stress and worry come from an excess of energy in your physical, mental, and emotional bodies, so by using black kyanite to remove the energetic debris, you can clear your energy field and calm your physical body. Begin at the top of your head, and holding the kyanite like a comb, sweep any negativity down toward the earth. Cleanse your crystal thoroughly when you're finished.

# Larvikite

APPEARANCE/COLOR: Gray with flecks of black and reflective silvery blue
CURRENT AVAILABILITY: Uncommon, but available from specialty stores
PHYSIOLOGICAL CORRESPONDENCE: Endocrine system, brain
PSYCHOLOGICAL CORRESPONDENCE: Mental stability, inner strength
KEYWORDS: Shungite, black moonstone, indigo gabbro
Keywords: Foundation, order, psychic protection

## The Crystal

Larvikite (also known as silver labradorite or pearl granite) originally comes from Larvik, Norway and is quite uncommon. It is a variety of the rock monzonite.

## Legendary Uses

Primarily used as a building material and marketed under the name pearl granite, larvikite is just starting to be available in the mineral and jewelry market. Larvikite has no known historical associations.

## Attributes and Powers

Larvikite is quite a mystical stone. It is excellent for protecting the energy body and makes a useful companion for journey work and astral projection. This crystal can also help you to take notice of your shadow side and change those parts of yourself that require emotional and spiritual growth. Larvikite creates a strong foundation and provides you with mental stability during difficult situations. It acts as a pillar of strength, supporting and protecting you during times of transformation and deep personal growth. Larvikite also reminds you to go with the flow and not fight against the currents of change. Larvikite crystals can help you to be flexible and willing to accept new things into your life for the highest good of all involved.

### HOW TO USE

Larvikite is useful when added to a protective medicine pouch. It can also be used to create a simple protective grid by placing a stone in each corner of a room. When creating this larvikite grid, you should set an intention that the stone's energy help to support and protect you. You may keep this intention general, but it's best to be as specific as possible in relation to your unique situation.

# Libyan Desert Glass

APPEARANCE/COLOR: Transparent; pale yellow to soft gold

CURRENT AVAILABILITY: Rare, but available from some specialty stores

PHYSIOLOGICAL CORRESPONDENCE: Pancreas

PSYCHOLOGICAL CORRESPONDENCE: Cheerful, supportive

KEYWORDS: Citrine, bytownite, golden topaz

Keywords: Power, rebirth, confidence

## The Crystal

Libyan desert glass is a pale yellow to soft gold, glass-like tektite formed from a meteorite that impacted an area near the Great Sand Sea of Egypt's Western Desert. The exact impact site has not yet been located, so the origin of these stones is still highly disputed. The stones were thought to have formed between 26 million to 29 million years ago. Because it is a natural glass, called lechatelierite, it has no internal crystalline structure.

## Legendary Uses

Libyan desert glass was officially discovered and named in 1932, but can be seen in ancient Egyptian jewelry from thousands of years ago. A large Libyan desert glass scarab is set into the center of the Pharaoh Tutankhamun's pectoral brooch. The ancient Egyptians referred to this stone as "the Rock of God." Libyan desert glass may even have been used as long ago as 8,000 BCE to fashion basic tools and blades.

## Attributes and Powers

Libyan desert glass is a very high vibrational stone. It can be used to instill confidence and enhance feelings of personal power. It encourages you to lift yourself up by your own bootstraps when you're feeling down or are focused on self-pity rather than seeking solutions to problems. It helps connect you to the energy of the stars and gives you insight and wisdom from the divine. This crystal is a reminder that not all of the answers have to come from within yourself, but rather that the solutions you seek may occasionally require a shifting in external forces.

### HOW TO USE

Charge your stone in starlight by placing it on your windowsill overnight and carry it with you to absorb its vibrations.

# Obsidian (Gold Sheen)

**APPEARANCE/COLOR:** Opaque; glassy black with a gold schiller
**CURRENT AVAILABILITY:** Uncommon
**PHYSIOLOGICAL CORRESPONDENCE:** Skull, bones, blood
**PSYCHOLOGICAL CORRESPONDENCE:** Safety, security, compassion
**KEYWORDS:** Safety, security, compassion
Keywords: Protection, ancestors, grieving

## The Crystal

Gold sheen obsidian is a variety of obsidian that gets its characteristic golden schiller from mineral inclusions, rock debris, or gas molecules. Obsidian is a natural glass and has no internal crystalline structure; it's an amorphous mineral. The best quality golden sheen obsidian comes from Guatemala, but it has also been found in Mexico.

## Legendary Uses

There is a Mexican legend about a woman named Xochitzol, meaning "flower of the sun," who was separated from her love when he was sent off to war. She vowed to wait for him until his return. When much time had passed, Xochitzol realized that her mate was not going to return, so she began to cry. The gods, feeling pity for her, turned her tears to golden obsidian.

## Attributes and Powers

Gold sheen obsidian works with ancestor spirits to keep you safe and protected. The energy of the obsidian calls on your ancestors and invites them into your space so that they can watch over you and keep you free from harm. For this reason, it instills you with feelings of safety and security when you're using it. This stone is also used for healing after great loss and can assist you in the grieving process.

### HOW TO USE

Place a piece of gold sheen obsidian on your altar or in your sacred space along with photos of any family members who have crossed over to the other side. Invite your ancestors into your space, letting them know that they are welcome and ask them to keep you safe from harm. Offer to share the stone's energy them as a way to thank them for their protection and kindness.

# Pietersite

APPEARANCE/COLOR: Opaque, chatoyant blue, brown, red, and gold swirls
CURRENT AVAILABILITY: Limited availability
PHYSIOLOGICAL CORRESPONDENCE: Spine, stomach, brow
PSYCHOLOGICAL CORRESPONDENCE: Emotional boundaries, discernment
KEYWORDS: Blue tiger's eye, dumortierite, blue apatite
Keywords: Protection, shielding, space clearing

## The Crystal

Pietersite (also known as tempest stone) is a form of chalcedony that contains inclusions of crocidolite, a chatoyant mineral that gives pietersite its characteristic shimmer. Crocidolite is a variety of riebeckite and is part of the monoclinic crystal system. Pietersite is only found in two places on earth, Namibia and China, so it is relatively uncommon.

## Legendary Uses

This mineral was first described in 1962 by Sid Pieters. Because pietersite is so new to the mineral market, it does not have any associated legendary uses.

## Attributes and Powers

Pietersite is an immensely protective stone, shielding you from negative influences and people. This mineral acts like a cloak of invisibility when you need your space or distance from those who would otherwise drain your energy. Additionally, pietersite helps to clear your space if you're trapped in a negative place or environment. This crystal can be fierce with those who would seek to take advantage of you, but will take you under its wing to shield you from their cruelty or mistreatment. Pietersite also helps get to the core of negative relationship patterns so that you no longer have to repeat cycles of unhealthy behavior with your friends, your family members, or your romantic partners.

### HOW TO USE

If you know you're going to be somewhere with negative people or negative energy in the environment, slip a piece of pietersite into your pocket. Your crystal will shield you, like a cloak of invisibility, from difficult people and situations. Pietersite sends positive vibrations into the space, counteracting the negativity of others so that you don't feel overwhelmed by their energy.

# Quartz (Hollandite)

APPEARANCE/COLOR: Transparent; black starlike inclusions

CURRENT AVAILABILITY: Rare

PHYSIOLOGICAL CORRESPONDENCE: Teeth, veins, colon

PSYCHOLOGICAL CORRESPONDENCE: Neutrality, curiosity

KEYWORDS: Black Tibetan quartz, graphite quartz, brookite quartz

Keywords: Astral travel, cosmic consciousness, oneness

## The Crystal

Hollandite quartz is a variety of quartz crystal that contains small starburst-like inclusions of black hollandite. The tiny starbursts look almost like little spiders, which are responsible for the crystal's alternate names of spider quartz and star quartz. This special mineral combination only comes from Madagascar. Hollandite is a monoclinic crystal, while quartz is hexagonal or trigonal.

## Legendary Uses

Hollandite quartz has no known legendary or historical uses.

## Attributes and Powers

Hollandite quartz has a very unique energy. It helps to connect you to the universal source and experience oneness with all beings. Everything in this universe, including you, is born of stardust; hollandite quartz reminds you of your cosmic roots. This crystal facilitates astral travel and journeying, taking you to new depths of consciousness and states of mind. Hollandite quartz strengthens the grounding cord that keeps your ethereal and astral bodies in connection with your physical being. So even though this crystal may help to push you farther into the cosmic depths than is within your comfort zone, it also helps keep you safe on your journey.

### HOW TO USE

Place a piece of hollandite quartz on your bedside table or slip one inside your pillowcase to promote meaningful astral travel experiences. Place another of these crystals at the base of your bed near your feet to keep your astral body firmly anchored to your physical form. Bring your attention to your physical body and feel yourself connected to both stones. Set an intention for your cosmic journey and gently drift off to sleep while holding this intention in your mind.

# Shiva Lingam

APPEARANCE/COLOR: Opaque; mottled gray, tan, and deep brown
CURRENT AVAILABILITY: Common
PHYSIOLOGICAL CORRESPONDENCE: Pineal gland, phallus, DMT production
PSYCHOLOGICAL CORRESPONDENCE: Oneness
KEYWORDS: Print stone, petrified peanut wood, petrified wood
Keywords: Masculinity, formlessness, egolessness, love, spiritual surrender

## The Crystal

Shiva lingams (also called banalinga) are naturally formed, oblong, elliptical, rounded rocks found in the Narmada River in India.

## Legendary Uses

The term lingam is used to describe an oblong symbol for the Hindu god Shiva, but the actual lingam stones are referred to as banalinga and are used in Shiva worship. The construction of Hindu temples corresponds to the anatomy of the human body. The location of the revered lingam stone is placed in correspondence with the pineal gland in the human brain. There is a Hindu legend that tells the story of a great battle between Lord Brahma and Lord Vishnu. Lord Shiva decided to intervene in the battle, taking the form of a great lingam of fire. He challenged Brahma and Vishnu to find the ends of the column of fire, explaining that whoever reached the ends of his form first would be the greater of the two gods. Brahma took the form of a swan, flying up in the sky to search for one end of the fire lingam, while Vishnu took the form of a boar, tunneling into the earth to find the other. Neither was able to find the ends of the great pillar. Shiva reappeared to them, showing them that he could not be sought out from a place of ego, but only from a place of love and surrender. This tale shows that the lingam has no beginning and no end and that all in this world is both form and formless.

## Attributes and Powers

The Shiva lingam stone is a powerful ritual object. It represents formlessness and the dissolution of the ego mind. Use it to journey into the depths of your conscious awareness.

### HOW TO USE

Place your Shiva lingam stone in a place of prominence within your sacred space and meditate with it often.

# Staurolite

APPEARANCE/COLOR: Opaque; tan to brown
CURRENT AVAILABILITY: Somewhat common
PHYSIOLOGICAL CORRESPONDENCE: Heart, hands, feet, head
PSYCHOLOGICAL CORRESPONDENCE: Hope
KEYWORDS: Bronzite, golden tiger's eye, cross stone
Keywords: Mercy, protection, good luck

## The Crystal

Staurolite is a tan to brown mineral that forms cross-shaped twin crystals. The best quality twinned staurolite "crosses" come from Russia, but they can also be found in other countries. The specimens formed at perfect right angles are the most highly sought after, but staurolite may also form other interesting shapes like Xs or five- or six-pointed stars.

## Legendary Uses

This mineral is named for the Greek word **stauros**, meaning "cross," and **lithos**, meaning "stone." These crystals are also known as "faith crosses," "fairy crosses," or "fairy luck stones." One legend states that at the time of Christ's crucifixion, angels and fairies surrounded him and wept for his suffering. These tears fell to earth and formed staurolite. Another popular legend says that as the Cherokee people were forced to leave their homes and set out on the trail of tears, these stones were left behind as they wept. Another Cherokee legend describes the use of the staurolite stones during an annual ritual where the stones were heated in a great fire and would glow all night until the sun rose the next morning. This ceremony was thought to bring good luck, abundance, and safe travels. The Cherokee also associated these stones with the four elements. A Gaelic legend describes the formation of the stones as the tears the fairies wept when Tuatha de Danaan was defeated in ancient Ireland. These crystals were used in Swiss baptisms and were carried as good luck charms by three United States presidents.

## Attributes and Powers

Staurolite crystals balance the influence of the four elements on the body, keeping you balanced and protected.

---

### HOW TO USE

Place a staurolite crystal on your altar or in the center of a labyrinth or medicine wheel to amplify its protective and luck-bearing qualities.

# Topaz (Imperial Golden)

**APPEARANCE/COLOR:** Transparent; gold to peachy orange
**CURRENT AVAILABILITY:** Slightly uncommon
**PHYSIOLOGICAL CORRESPONDENCE:** Digestive system, spleen, pancreas
**PSYCHOLOGICAL CORRESPONDENCE:** Motivation, determination
**KEYWORDS:** Citrine, golden calcite, bytownite, amber
Keywords: Energizing, protective

## The Crystal

Imperial golden topaz is a member of the orthorhombic crystal system. It most commonly forms small, single-terminated points of gold to peachy orange color. The finest quality crystals come from Brazil, but they can also be found in Zambia. These stones may be heated or irradiated to intensify their color, so if you prefer a natural stone, be sure to buy from a reputable source.

## Legendary Uses

Imperial topaz is the November birthstone. The name topaz may come from the Sanskrit word **tapaz,** meaning "fire." The ancient Egyptians saw this gem as a symbol of the sun god Ra. Some historical sources claim that this stone would change colors if it were placed near poisons, so it was coveted by kings and queens who feared treason and deceit.

## Attributes and Powers

Imperial golden topaz is one of the finest semiprecious gemstones in the world. Its brilliant golden color corresponds to the fire element, instilling a sense of motivation and determination. This attribute influences the stone's ability to burn up negative energy from within the aura. It is a highly protective crystal. Imperial golden topaz resonates with the solar plexus chakra and can energize your physical and subtle bodies. By keeping your field full of positive energy, it becomes more difficult for others to create energetic cords or attachments to your field.

### HOW TO USE

Wearing an imperial golden topaz pendant on a long chain over your solar plexus chakra is very beneficial for keeping you energized, but wearing the stone set in a pair of earrings can help you maintain a sunny disposition.

# Tourmaline (Blue)

APPEARANCE/COLOR: Transparent; pale blue, to bright blue, to deep indigo

CURRENT AVAILABILITY: Limited availability

PHYSIOLOGICAL CORRESPONDENCE: Cardiovascular system

PSYCHOLOGICAL CORRESPONDENCE: Relaxation, calmness

KEYWORDS: Blue kyanite, blue sapphire, afghanite

Keywords: Intuition, psychic protection, energy shield

## The Crystal

Blue tourmaline is a trigonal crystal with sub-varieties including elbaite and indicolite. It forms striated crystals, typically in small clusters or large single points. It is found in many locations across the globe, but the highest quality pieces are from Brazil and Namibia.

## Legendary Uses

Ancient Romans carved various animal figures out of blue tourmaline. There is an Egyptian legend about how tourmaline acquired its variety of colors. The legend states that tourmaline journeyed along a rainbow as it moved from the center of the earth to try and get nearer to the sun. Along the way, the stone absorbed all of the colors of the rainbow.

## Attributes and Powers

Blue tourmaline is associated with the Tibetan Buddhist goddess, Blue Tara (named Ekajati). Blue Tara represents inner peace and is known for cooling the flames of anger. Blue tourmaline invokes these qualities and helps you to calm fiery emotions and find your center. Blue tourmaline, like Blue Tara, is a fierce protector and will work to keep you safe at all costs. Blue tourmaline also encourages spiritual growth and helps removes obstacles from your path to enlightenment and spiritual awakening. This crystal can also be used as a good luck charm.

### HOW TO USE

To invite the energy of the Blue Tara goddess into your crystal to help you on your path to spiritual awakening, place your crystal on the eye of a peacock feather. Ask the goddess for wisdom and insight about what needs to be fully realized on your spiritual journey. Sit in quiet meditation and await a response in the stillness.

# Ulexite

APPEARANCE/COLOR: Transparent clear to translucent white; rarely pale gray

CURRENT AVAILABILITY: Common

PHYSIOLOGICAL CORRESPONDENCE: Eyes, brain, muscles

PSYCHOLOGICAL CORRESPONDENCE: Secrecy, truthfulness, integrity, honesty

KEYWORDS: Selenite, petalite, scolecite

Keywords: Hidden messages, revelation, heroism

## The Crystal

Ulexite is a member of the triclinic crystal system. It typically forms striated, white, fibrous masses, but it can also form tiny, needlelike clusters. The best quality ulexite stones are found in the United States, but the stone is widely available from other locations. There is an optical form of ulexite that is also known as "TV stone."

## Legendary Uses

Ulexite has no known legendary or historical uses.

## Attributes and Powers

Ulexite works like a window to the soul. It allows you to see your innermost truth. It can also be used to reveal hidden messages or that which is being kept from you. Use ulexite to shine a light on deceitful people in your life or to reveal those who are not being truthful with you. This stone is also helpful for exposing secrets that, if kept, will negatively impact those who you care about.

### HOW TO USE

Gather together a ulexite stone, a pen or pencil, and some scraps of paper. Make yourself comfortable in your sacred space and ponder a situation where you suspect someone is being intentionally deceitful. Write down the names of each person involved in the situation, each on a separate scrap of paper. Hold the ulexite over each person's name and attempt to read the names through the ulexite stone. Those that come through very clearly are being honest and transparent with you, while those whose names appear dull or cloudy are most likely hiding something of importance.

**The Beginner's Guide to Crystal Healing**

# Index